Arts & Crafts for Home Decorating®

GARDEN ORNAMENTS

Stylish Projects to Complement Your Garden

The Home Decorating Institute®

CREATIVE PUBLISHING international
MINNETONKA, MINNESOTA

President/CEO: David D. Murphy
Vice President/Editorial:
Patricia K. Jacobsen
Vice President/Retail Sales & Marketing:
Richard M. Miller

GARDEN ORNAMENTS
Created by: The Editors of
Creative Publishing international, Inc.

Books available in this series:
Bedroom Decorating, Creative Window Treatments, Decorating for Christmas, Decorating the Living Room, Creative Accessories for the Home, Decorating with Silk & Dried Flowers, Kitchen & Bathroom Ideas, Decorating the Kitchen, Decorative Painting, Decorating Your Home for Christmas, Decorating for Dining & Entertaining, Decorating with Fabric & Wallcovering, Decorating the Bathroom, Decorating with Great Finds, Affordable Decorating, Picture-Perfect Walls, More Creative Window Treatments, Outdoor Decor, The Gift of Christmas, Home Accents in a Flash, Painted Illusions, Halloween Decorating, 'Tis the Season

Printed by R. R. Donnelley & Sons Co.
10 9 8 7 6 5 4 3 2 1

Creative Publishing international, Inc. offers a variety of how-to books. For information write:
Creative Publishing international, Inc.
Subscriber Books
5900 Green Oak Drive
Minnetonka, MN 55343

Contents

Welcome

Welcome

This book was in my heart and on my mind for almost a year before it reached the drawing board. During that time, I was so interested in designing and building garden ornaments that they jumped out at me from every direction. Every antique, curio, and objet d'art I saw, whether in a store, catalog, art fair, or neighbor's yard, had a detail that I wanted to adapt or include in one of the projects growing in my imagination. I spent most of one winter puttering, testing designs, and playing with ideas.

That period of near obsession provided a base of material that Tim Himsel and his talented team of designers, photographers, and artists brought to life in ways that exceeded my fondest imaginings. Developing this book was one of the most joyous experiences of my life, and it gives me great pleasure to welcome you to its pages and to the delight of building garden ornaments.

Perhaps you have a fairly well-established garden, one with trees, shrubs, perennials, and pathways largely in place. Or perhaps, like me, you have a long-term plan for your yard and are bringing individual areas to completion before moving on. In either case, if you're reading this book, you're probably ready to add ornaments and accessories to your landscape and garden.

Some of the projects you'll find here require carpentry skills, and others require a little dexterity, but they're all well within the capabilities of any motivated gardener with access to simple building materials and a few power tools.

Each project includes a list of tools and materials, dimensions, and detailed building instructions, but don't hesitate to adapt and alter a project to suit your own garden. Whenever possible, I've added variations to help you adapt these ideas to suit your own garden. You may want to enlarge a project or adapt the materials to suit the style, theme, or colors in your garden. In fact, before you purchase materials or begin building, it's a good idea to spend some time envisioning the project in place and considering whether any modifications are necessary.

The best advice I can give you is this: Let your imagination run wild. Follow your instincts, and trust your own sense of style—if you build and buy only ornaments you truly love, they'll come together to create a beautiful garden that's uniquely your own.

Teri Harris

Water Features

This chapter is my personal favorite. I'm drawn to water in any form and, like many people, find the sound of running water soothing and refreshing. Water features are everywhere these days—from garden centers to Buddhist boutiques—but most of them carry fairly hefty price tags. With any of the projects in this chapter, it's possible to bring the delights of water into your garden at a very reasonable cost. You can have a great deal of fun in the process, too: Every one of these projects is a joy to build.

Water features offer tremendous opportunities to express creativity. For example, you can easily build an attractive terra cotta fountain (page 8) by following the instructions to the letter. Or, by selecting other types of vessels, stones, and plants, you can create a fountain that reflects your own personal style and taste. Similarly, the stone, spray pattern and plantings you choose for a cobblestone fountain (page 20) will make it uniquely your own.

If you want to attract attention to your yard and garden, there are few better ways than building a copper sprinkler (page 16). Honestly, people come to a complete stop to watch mine throw its graceful sprays across the garden. If you live on a highly-traveled street, be careful not to create a traffic hazard with yours.

Despite being remarkably easy to put together, the water garden variation (page 15) draws a good deal of attention as well. A small, relatively inexpensive device sends mist rolling from behind the decorations, creating a hypnotic, mysterious effect. You'll find a source for the mist device listed in Resources (page 111).

IN THIS CHAPTER:

Terra Cotta Fountains

Small fountains are quite popular, but the prices put them out of reach for many gardeners. But with our designs, you can bring the soothing sounds of trickling water to your garden easily and inexpensively. Assembling these terra cotta fountains is amazingly quick—you can shop for the materials and complete a fountain in just one day.

Purchase a small submersible pump with a flow rate of about 60 gallons per hour; then select a base container that's deep enough to submerge the water intake portion of the pump. Also, make sure the flexible tubing you purchase fits the pump's discharge outlet.

Choose smooth, uniform terra cotta pieces for these fountains. As you purchase pots, assemble them approximately as they'll be positioned in the completed fountain to make sure they stack evenly.

You can buy stones to place in the fountain, but if you live near a river or lake shore, it might be more fun to gather them. Smooth river stones will look more natural and appropriate in the fountain than sharp or jagged stones.

Check the water level in the fountain frequently. When a fountain, especially a small one, is operated in dry weather, rapid evaporation makes it necessary to replenish the water every two or three days. If possible, purchase a pump that shuts itself off when the water level falls below a set point. This feature keeps the pump from burning out if you can't refill the fountain for some reason.

In time, the clay pots in your fountain may develop a white residue caused by mineral deposits. To remove the stains, take the fountain apart and scrub each pot, using a nylon or natural-bristle brush. You can also rinse the pots with bleach to discourage the growth of mold, mildew, or algae.

TOOLS & MATERIALS

- Drill with 3/8" masonry bit and conical rasp bit
- 8" round bastard file
- Masking tape
- Clear aerosol acrylic sealer
- Ruler
- Permanent marker
- 5-gallon bucket
- Terra cotta saucers, one 18", one 8", one 6", and three 4"
- Terra cotta pots, one 6" and one 5"
- Submersible pump
- 12" length of flexible tubing
- Marine-grade sealant
- Embellishments, such as clean river rocks, gravel, coral or shells
- Small potted plants, candle, or small statue

HOW TO MAKE A TERRA COTTA FOUNTAIN

Step A: Prepare the Pottery

1. Put masking tape around the outside of the upper edge of the 18" saucer to protect the edges from overspray. Spray a coat of acrylic sealer on the inside of the saucer and let it dry. Apply two more coats of sealer to the interior of the saucer and let them dry.

2. Center and mark an X on the bottom of the 8" saucer, using a ruler and permanent marker. Place this saucer and the 6" pot, the 6" saucer, and two 4" saucers in a bucket of water; let them soak for at least an hour.

3. Position the 8" saucer over a scrap of wood and drill a hole at the X, using a 3/8" masonry drill bit. Test-fit the flexible plastic tubing and enlarge the hole, if necessary, using a conical rasp bit. Drill slowly while applying light pressure, and check the fit at frequent intervals. The flexible plastic tubing should fit snugly through the hole in the saucer.

4. Use the drill to adjust the hole in the bottom of the 6" pot until the flexible plastic tubing fits snugly through it as well. Using a round bastard file, cut four notches in the lip of the pot, sizing one notch to accommodate the electrical cord of the pump.

5. File one notch for a water spout in the edge of the 8" saucer, using a round bastard file. To create the best water flow, angle the notch toward the inside edge of the saucer, leaving the outer lip of the notch higher than the inner edge.

6. File an angled notch in the 6" saucer and in one 4" saucer.

7. File four notches equally spaced around the upper edge of another 4" saucer.

Step B: Attach the Pump

1. Connect the flexible plastic tubing to the discharge outlet of the pump. If it's difficult to slide the

A. *File four notches in the lip of the 6" pot. Make one of the notches large enough to accommodate the pump's cord.*

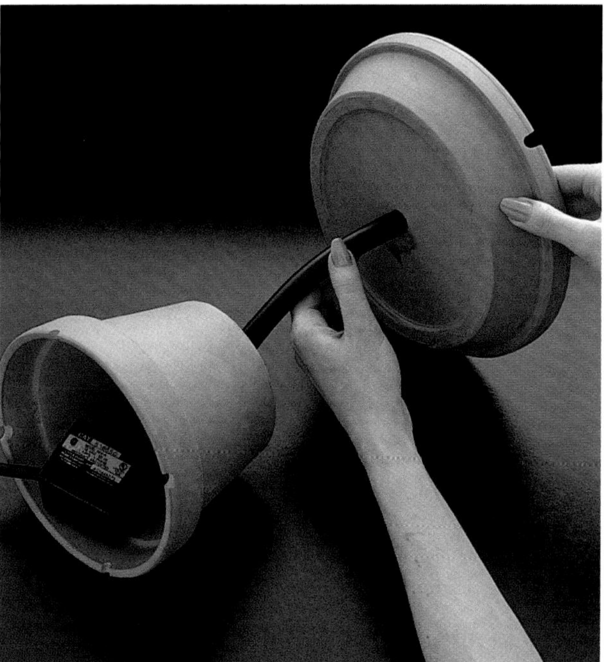

B. *Connect one end of the tubing to the discharge outlet of the pump; then insert the other through the inverted pot and saucer.*

tubing over the outlet, place the end of the tubing in hot water for a minute or two; then try again.

2. Turn the 6" pot upside down and insert the free end of the tubing through the pot, then through the 8" saucer to create the tallest column of the fountain.

Step C: Position the First Column

1. Pull the flexible plastic tubing up through the saucer until it's taut, and then trim it, leaving about ½" of tubing above the saucer. Use marine-grade sealant to seal gaps between the tubing and the saucer. Let the sealant cure, following manufacturer's instructions.

2. Place the pump and column in the 18" base saucer. Adjust the pump's electrical cord to fit through the notch you cut for it in the lip of the pot. Find the 4" saucer with four notches; place it upside down in the center of the 8" saucer, concealing the tubing.

Step D: Arrange Remaining Columns

1. Turn the 5" pot upside down and position it in the base saucer, next to the first column.

2. Place the notched 6" saucer on top of the pot, forming the middle column.

3. Turn the unnotched 4" saucer upside down and place it in the base saucer; place the notched 4" saucer on top, creating the short column.

Step E: Add Water & Embellish the Fountain

1. Fill the base with water, adding more water until it's about ⅜" from the rim of the saucer. Turn on the pump and check the flow of the water.

2. Adjust the position of the notched saucers until water pours smoothly from one column of the fountain to the next.

3. Adjust the flow rate of the pump, if necessary, to achieve a smooth, even flow of water.

4. Add clean rocks, gravel, coral, or shells to the saucers as desired.

5. Place a potted plant, candle, or small statue on top of the tallest column to weight down the inverted saucer and add the finishing touch to your terra cotta fountain. Position a second potted plant in the base saucer, if desired.

C. *Pull the flexible plastic tubing up through the saucer until it's taut, trim it, and seal any gaps with marine sealant.*

D. *Stack the middle column and place it in the base saucer. Top an inverted, unnotched 4" saucer with a notched saucer, creating a short column.*

E. *Fill the fountain with water and run the pump. Adjust the position of the columns and the pump's flow rate until the water flows smoothly from one level to another.*

VARIATION: STRAWBERRY POT FOUNTAIN

You can make another simple, attractive fountain by topping a stack of standard pots with a strawberry pot. Again, you use a small pump to recirculate water through the stack, sending a graceful flow out of the openings of the strawberry pot and down the stack.

For this fountain, you'll need the same general supplies as for the Terra Cotta Fountain. You'll also need:

- 15" base container or saucer
- 10" pot
- 8" saucer
- 10" strawberry pot
- Duct tape
- Plaster of Paris.

If there's a drainage hole in the base container, fill it with plaster of Paris. Working from the bottom of the container, put duct tape across the hole. Mix a small amount of plaster of Paris, following manufacturer's instructions. Fill about half of the hole with plaster and let it harden. Repeat to fill the remainder of the hole. When the plaster is dry, seal the interior of the bowl (page 9).

Mark the center of the strawberry pot and the 8" saucer; soak both of them and the 10" pot in water for at least an hour. Drill a hole in the saucer (page 9); then drill or enlarge the hole in the strawberry pot to fit the discharge tube of the water pump.

File notches in the base pot, and drill holes in the pottery. Stack the pieces and position the water pump and its tube.

File four equally spaced notches in the upper edge of the 10" pot, using a round bastard file. Size one of the notches to accommodate the electrical cord of the pump.

Connect the flexible plastic tubing to the pump (page 9). Turn the 10" pot upside down and insert the free end of the tubing through the pot and the saucer, and then through the bottom of the strawberry pot.

Position the pump and stacked pottery in the base container and fit the pump's electrical cord through the appropriate notch. Pull the flexible plastic tubing taut and use marine sealant to seal any gaps between the tubing and the strawberry pot. Allow the sealant to cure, following the manufacturer's instructions.

Fill the strawberry pot with about 3" of gravel; keep the flexible plastic tubing centered in the pot. Trim the tubing, leaving about ½" above the surface of the gravel.

Add water to the base container until it reaches within about ⅜" of the container's rim. Plug in the pump and adjust the flow rate as necessary. Place gravel, rocks, or shells in the rim of the saucer and base, if desired. Add a potted plant to the top of the strawberry pot.

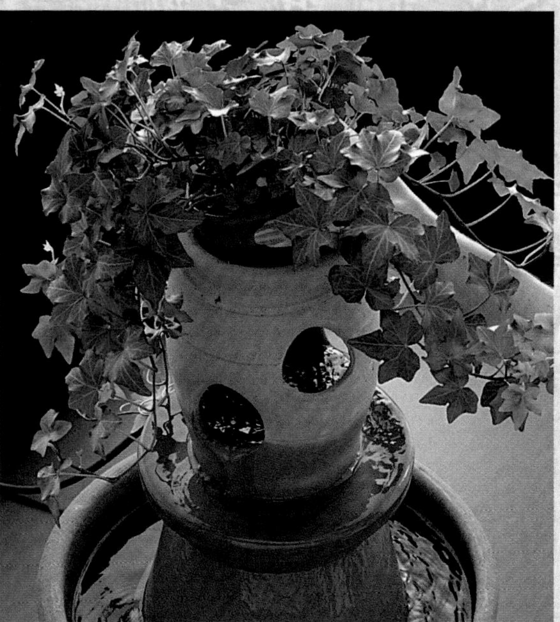

Position the stacked pots in the base saucer; then add gravel, water, and plants.

Water Gardens

Water gardens add a dreamy, peaceful feeling to quiet spaces. If, like me, you don't have the space or time to maintain a formal pond, you might have the perfect spot on a deck or patio or in a boring corner of the yard for this simple, easy-to-build water garden.

Almost any vessel that holds water can be turned into a water garden, but some materials work better than others. One of the best ideas I've found is to start with a vinyl all-purpose tub, and then build a cedar surround to give it a finished appearance.

All-purpose tubs are available at most building supply stores, farm supply stores, and pet supply stores. Measure the tub you select; then purchase cedar lumber that's at least as wide as the depth of the tub, probably 1 × 12s or 1 × 10s.

Although it's not required, a small spray is a nice addition. Buy a small submersible pump with a fountain head attachment. A pump with a flow rate of 80 gallons per hour will create a fountain spray about 10" high, which suits a water garden of this size quite nicely.

Many nurseries stock a large variety of aquatic plants, but they're also available from mail-order sources. Aquatic plants include those that grow in containers of soil submerged beneath the surface of the water as well as floating plants, whose roots dangle in the water. The chart on page 14 lists several commonly available aquatic plants.

Many traditional potted plants and flowering plants can be placed in water gardens if the pots are only partially submerged. Floating pond plants block the sunlight from the water, which helps reduce algae growth. To further reduce the growth of algae, periodically replace the water in the garden.

To create a more interesting arrangement, select plants in a variety of textures and heights. Keep in mind, though, that plants should cover no more than three-fourths of the water's surface.

TOOLS & MATERIALS

- Circular saw or jig saw
- Drill with countersink bit
- Paintbrush
- Tape measure
- Large vinyl tub
- 1 × 12 or 1 × 10 cedar lumber
- 1 × 2 cedar lumber
- #6 × 2" galvanized deck screws
- Wood sealer
- Submersible pump
- Aquatic plants
- Pea gravel
- Bricks or clay saucers

A. *Align the front and one side; then drill three counterbored pilot holes. Drive screws to fasten the pieces.*

HOW TO BUILD A WATER GARDEN

Step A: Assemble the Frame

1. Measure the width of the vinyl tub from the outside edges. Add ½", then measure, mark, and cut two 1 × 12s or 1 × 10s to this adjusted measurement. These pieces will form the sides of the surround.

2. Measure the outer length of the tub and add 2". Cut two pieces to this length to form the front and back of the frame.

3. Lightly sand the edges and ends of the cut boards as necessary. Drill a notch at one end of the back piece, placed near the lower edge, to accommodate the pump's electrical cord.

4. Apply wood sealer to both faces and to the edges of the boards. Allow them to dry completely.

5. Align the front piece with a side piece. Drill three pilot holes, using a countersink bit. Drive screws into the pilot holes, fastening the front to the side. Repeat for the remaining side, then for the back.

Step B: Add the Casings

1. Measure the length of the box. Add ½", then measure, mark, and cut two pieces of 1 × 2 to this length. These pieces will form the front and back casings.

2. Set the front and back casings in place, centering each over the frame and extending ¼" beyond the ends of the frame. Measure the frame between the front and back casings, and cut two pieces of 1 × 2 to this length for the side casings.

3. Apply wood sealer to all the edges and cut ends of the casing pieces. Allow them to dry.

4. Realign the front casing, making sure it's centered on the frame. Drill three counterbored pilot holes; then secure the casing to the frame, using deck screws. Repeat with the back casing.

B. *Center the casing on top of the frame, extending it ½" beyond the inside edge. Drill counterbored pilot holes; then fasten the casing with screws.*

C. *Place the tub in the surround. If necessary, use boards or bricks to bring the tub up to within ½" of the top of the surround.*

5. Center one side casing between the front and back casings. Drill counterbored pilot holes; then drive screws to fasten the casing to the frame. Repeat on the opposite side.

Step C: Install the Tub and Surround

Place the tub inside the surround. If necessary, use boards or bricks to elevate the tub to within ½" of the top of the surround.

Step D: Install the Pump & Fountain Head

Position a submersible pump in the tub. Run the electrical cord over the edge of the tub, under the surround, and through the notch you drilled for it. Fill the tub with water, turn on the pump, and adjust the flow rate of the pump to create an effect that appeals to you.

Step E: Embellish the Garden

1. Place pea gravel on top of the soil in potted plants; then position them in the tub. Use inverted terra cotta pots, saucers, or bricks to adjust each plant to its recommended water depth, as indicated on the nursery tag. Set taller plants in position to camouflage the spot where the electrical cord is draped over the tub.

2. Arrange floating plants to balance the appearance of the water garden.

TYPES OF AQUATIC PLANTS

CONTAINER PLANT		FLOATING PLANTS
Arrowhead	Spike rush	Parrot feather
Canna	Variegated sweet flag	Water hyacinth
Cattail	Water iris	Water lettuce
Dwarf papyrus	Water lilies	
Lizard tail umbrella palm		

D. *Place the pump in the tub. Add water; then adjust the flow rate to create a pleasing effect.*

E. *Arrange potted and floating plants in the water garden.*

VARIATION: FOUNTAIN GARDENS

BARREL WATER GARDEN

You can create simple, attractive water gardens in purchased containers. For the water garden (below, left), you need:

- Oak whiskey barrel
- Marine-grade sealant
- Rubber spatula
- 4d finish nails
- Submersible pump with fountain head attachment
- Floating and potted aquatic plants.

Scrub and rinse the interior of the barrel to remove any acids or alcohol residue. Let it dry.

Using a hammer, tap along the inside of the barrel to make sure the base is snug against the sides. Drive nails through the base, angling them into, but not through, the sides of the barrel.

Spread marine-grade sealant liberally around the inside of the barrel, particularly the side seams and any nail holes. Let the sealant dry; then apply a second coat and let it dry thoroughly.

Put the barrel in place and fill it with water. Use clean bricks, blocks, or clay pots to elevate the pump and plants.

MIST WATER GARDEN

Although it's amazingly easy to put together, this water garden (below, right), simply commands attention. The fog maker device, which works much like an ultrasonic humidifier, creates a mist that's almost mesmerizing (source listed on page 111). To create this water garden, you need:

- Ceramic container
- Mist maker fountain head
- Decorative accents.

Fill the base with water and place the mist maker about 1½" under the surface of the water. The mist effect changes with the amount of water covering the device, so adjust its position until the mist rises in a way that appeals to you. Note: *With containers larger than 20" in diameter, it may be necessary to use more than one fog maker to create the desired effect.*

Arrange stones, a small statue, or a miniature plant in the water garden.

Place the transformer portion of the fog maker in a sheltered area to protect it from the weather.

Check the water level often and refill as necessary. Do not leave the pump running if you'll be away from home for an extended period.

Left. *A whiskey barrel can become an inexpensive, attractive water garden.* **Above.** *A mist maker and a few accessories transform a piece of pottery into a unique water garden.*

Copper Sprinkler

Even when standing still, this sprinkler is an artistic addition to any yard or garden. In motion, it's utterly fascinating. As the hoop spins, it throws shimmering spirals that water an area as large as 15 ft. in diameter.

Despite the impressive results, this is an inexpensive project. Some of the parts come from unexpected sources, but they're all widely available. You can find copper pipe and fittings at virtually any home center. We found round brass tubing (made by K&S Engineering) at a hobby and crafts store, and the bushings at an auto parts store. We used hinge pin bushings made by Motormite, which worked well and fit nearly perfectly. They're GM replacement parts, so they should be easy to find.

We found that flexible copper bends more easily when it's new, and that building a bending jig helps you create a uniform circle, which distributes the weight evenly and allows the hoop to spin smoothly.

Spacing the holes is mildly tricky, but not complicated if you understand the concept. To create the directional force that makes the head spin, the holes must gradually move from the front side of the hoop to the back side. As water is pushed out the holes, the pressure rotates the hoop.

This sprinkler has a simple motif, but the project lends itself to adaptation. You're sure to come up with a dozen variations you'd like to try. Go ahead—copper sprinklers are fun to build, they make wonderful gifts, and the materials are inexpensive.

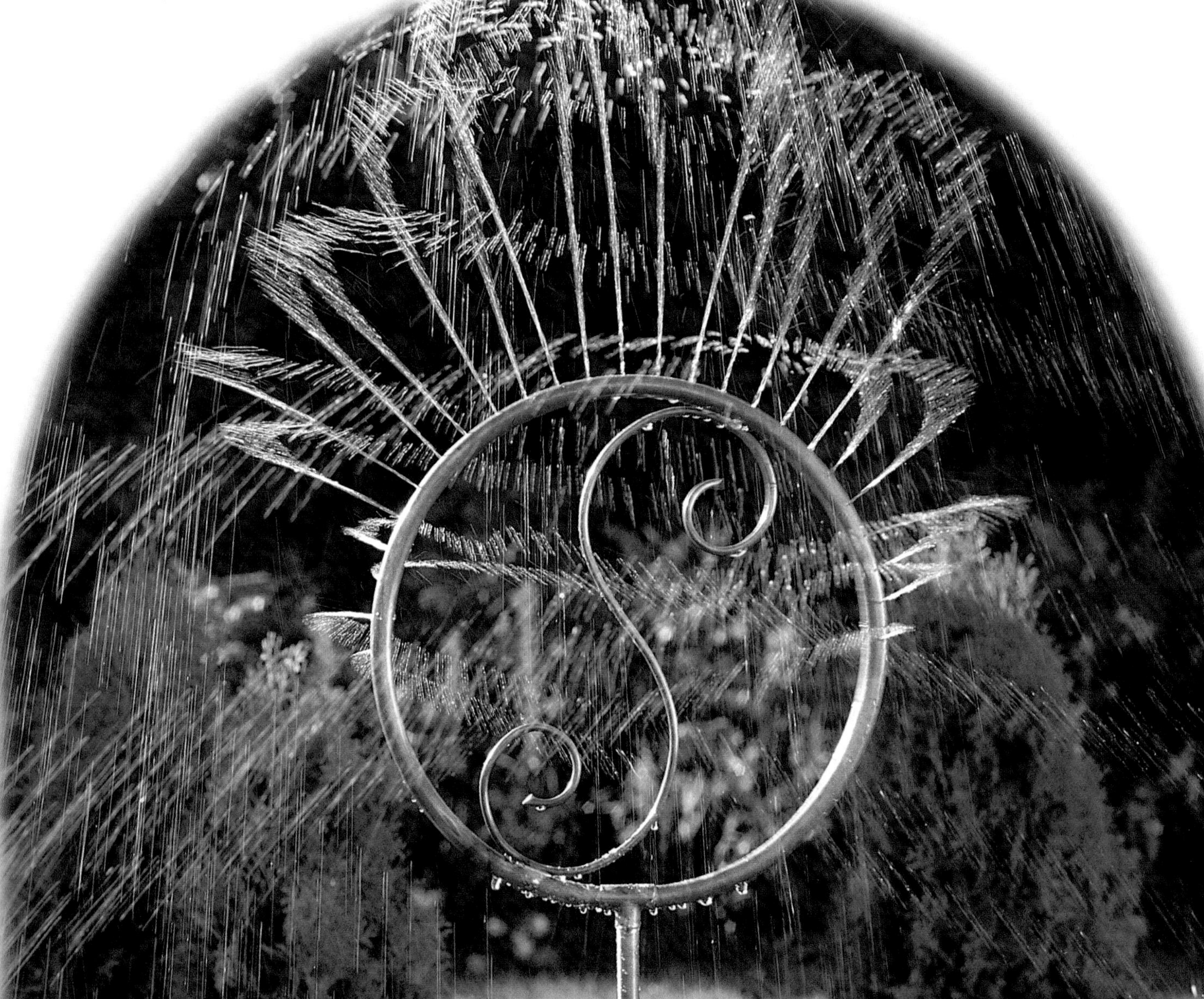

TOOLS & MATERIALS

- Tubing cutter
- Wire brush or emery cloth
- Bench grinder or rotary tool
- Flux brush
- Propane torch
- Circular saw
- Jig saw
- Drill
- 11/32" round brass tubing
- 5/16" round brass tubing
- Brass hinge pin bushings (GM #38375) (4)
- Flux
- Solder
- ½" flexible copper tubing, about 3 ft.
- ½" Type L copper pipe, about 4 ft.
- ¼" flexible copper tubing, 2 ft.
- ½" copper tee
- Two scraps of plywood (16" square)
- 1" deck screws (8)
- Cotton twine
- Permanent marker
- 6" galvanized wicket
- ½" brass shower ell
- ½" copper threaded adapter
- Teflon tape
- Machine screws & nuts (2)
- Metallic copper spray paint
- Brass hose connector

1/2" flexible copper tubing

1/2 x 5" Type L copper pipe

1/4" copper tubing

Hoop

1/2" tee

11/32 x 2" brass tube

Swivel joint

3/8" I.D. brass hinge pin bushing

1/2" copper pipe

5/16 x 6" brass tube

1/2" brass shower ell

11/32 x 4" brass tube

Upper Assembly

Bushing flange

6" iron wicket

1/2 x 36" Type L copper pipe

Lower Assembly

SWIVEL JOINT DETAILS

HOW TO BUILD A COPPER SPRINKLER

Step A: Make Assemblies for the Swivel Joint

1. Cut one 5" piece and one 36" piece of ½" Type L copper pipe, using a tubing cutter. Also cut one 2" and one 4" piece of 11/32" brass tubing, and one 6" piece of 5/16" brass tubing. Deburr the pieces, being careful not to flare the ends; use a wire brush or emery cloth to polish the ends.

2. Test-fit the hinge pin bushings inside the 5" piece of copper. If necessary, use a bench grinder or a

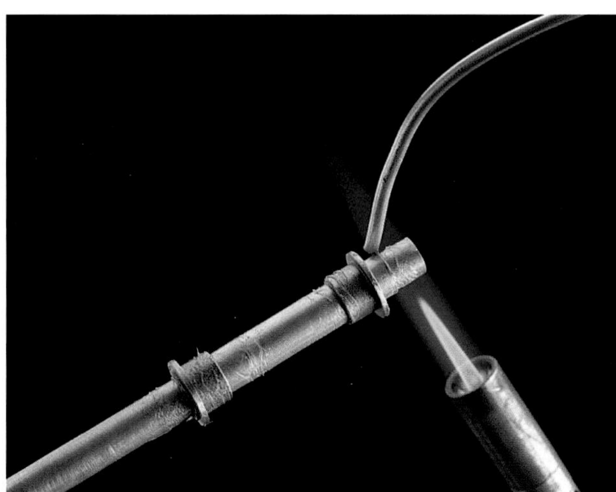

***A.** Solder upper assembly, connecting the 5/16" tube, the 11/32" tube, and the bushing. Heat all three pieces; first feed solder into the joint between the brass tubes, then into the bushing joint.*

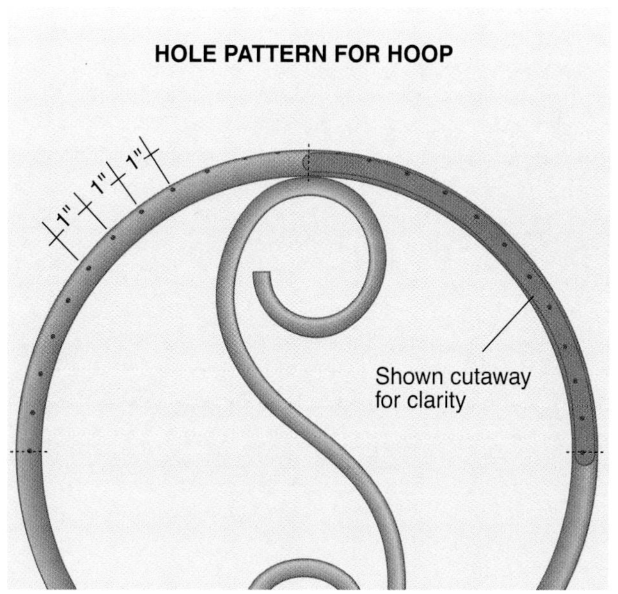

rotary tool to slightly shape the flanges of the hinge pin bushings so they fit snugly within the pipe. Note: *Using a scrap of the 11/32" tubing as a spindle helps you get a uniform edge.*

3. To form the upper assembly, slide a bushing onto each end of the 2" length of 11/32" brass tubing, with the flanges facing the ends of the tube. Set the flange of one bushing back 1/8" from the end of the tube; position the other bushing flush with the opposite end. Slide the 6" length of 5/16" brass tubing inside the 11/32" tube, positioning the inner tube to protrude 3/8" beyond the top (setback) bushing.

4. To form the lower assembly, slide a bushing onto

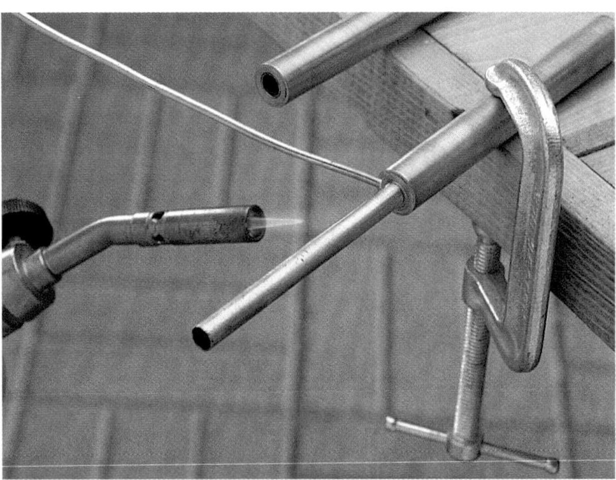

B. *Place the upper and lower assemblies of the swivel joint at the edge of a work surface, and solder the joints. To avoid letting solder run into the brass tubes, feed the solder from the bottom.*

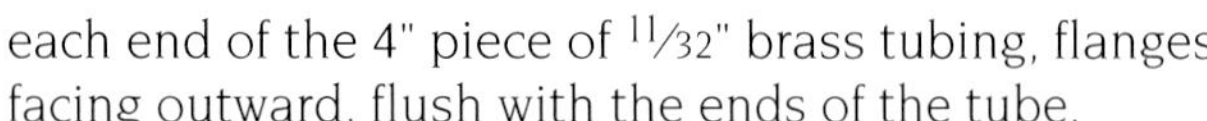

each end of the 4" piece of 11/32" brass tubing, flanges facing outward, flush with the ends of the tube.

5. Begin soldering at the top of the upper assembly (see page 100 for soldering techniques). Heat all three pieces—the 5/16" tube, the 11/32" tube, and the bushing. Feed solder into the joint between the two brass tubes first; feed solder into the bushing joint, approaching that joint from the side opposite the flange.

6. Solder the three remaining bushing joints, each time feeding the solder into the joint from the side opposite the flange.

Step B: Construct the Swivel Joint

1. Flux the inside of the 5" piece of 1/2" copper and the flange of the bushing on the upper assembly. Slide the assembly inside the copper pipe, positioning the lower bushing to be flush with the end of the copper pipe.

2. Flux the inside of the 36" piece of copper and the shoulder of one bushing on the lower assembly. Slide the assembly inside the pipe, positioning the bushing flange to be flush with the top of the pipe.

3. Place the assembled pieces at the edge of a protected work surface, and solder each one, being careful not to displace the bushings. Concentrate the flame on the copper pipe as you heat the joints, and feed the solder from the bottom; don't let the solder run into the brass tube.

Step C: Form the Hoop

1. To create a bending jig, cut two 16" squares from scrap plywood. Centered on one of the squares, mark concentric circles, one 13" and one 14 1/8" in diameter. Using a jig saw, cut out the inner circle, and then cut

C. *Build a plywood bending jig; then shape flexible copper tubing into a circle for the hoop.*

D. *Mark the placement of the holes and drill them along the hoop. (Be sure to drill through only one wall of the hoop.)*

along the line marking the outer circle.

2. Secure the 13" circle to the other plywood square, using 1" deck screws. Next, attach the outer edge of the cutout, centering it around the circle to form a channel that will guide the flexible tubing as you bend it into a hoop. Measure and mark lines dividing the circles into exact quarters.

3. Cut a generous length of ½" flexible copper tubing. Place one end in the channel, and then push the tubing into the jig, bending it down into the channel and around the inner circle as smoothly as possible. Mark and cut the tubing at the point where the ends meet. With the joint exactly lined up at the lower quarter mark on the jig, mark the other quarters on the tubing.

4. Remove the hoop from the jig, and add a ½" copper tee to one end. Bring the other end of the hoop around to the center of the tee, mark a cutting line, then cut the tubing.

5. Clean the cut ends and the tee, using a wire brush or emery cloth, and then flux the mating surfaces. Solder the tee in place.

Step D: Drill the Holes

1. Use a piece of twine to mark the curving pattern for the holes (diagram, page 17). Hold one end of the twine on the quarter mark on one side of the hoop. Pull the twine around the top of the hoop and down to the quarter mark on the opposite side.

2. Stretch the twine taut to create a smooth, curving line, and then transfer the quarter marks to the twine. Remove the twine and mark it at 1" intervals between the two quarter marks.

3. Wrap the string around the hoop, as before, aligning the quarter marks on the twine with those on the hoop to create a smooth curve. Tape the twine in place, and then use it as a pattern to mark the 1" intervals on the tubing. Drill a hole through one wall of the hoop at each mark.

Step E: Add the Swivel Joint & the Design Motif

1. Dry-fit the upper assembly of the swivel joint to the tee at the bottom of the hoop (be sure the brass tube is extending down). Flux mating surfaces and solder the joint.

2. Measure the inside diameter of the hoop, and then bend ¼" flexible copper tubing into an S shape to fit within the hoop (see page 17). You can alter the design if you wish, but keep in mind that its weight must be evenly distributed in order for the hoop to spin smoothly. Flux the appropriate spots and solder the design motif in place.

Step F: Build the Stand & Assemble the Sprinkler

1. Center a ½" brass shower ell on top of a 6" galvanized wicket, and mark the holes. Drill holes in the wicket, and then secure the ell to it, using machine screws and nuts. Spray paint these pieces to match the copper color of the sprinkler. Let the paint dry.

2. Solder a ½" threaded copper adapter to the open end of the stand pipe. When the piece is cool, wrap the threads of the adapter with Teflon tape. Screw the adapter into one end of the shower ell and a hose connector to the other.

3. Set the hoop into the stand pipe, mating the upper and lower portions of the swivel joint. Attach a garden hose to the hose connector.

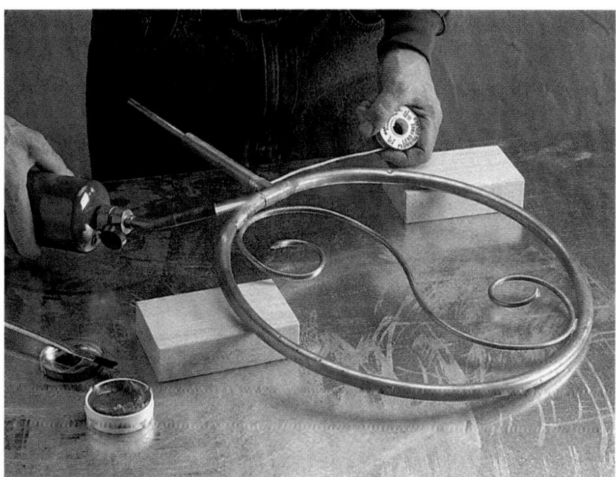

E. *Solder the swivel joint to the tee at the base of the hoop, and then form and solder the design motif to the interior of the hoop.*

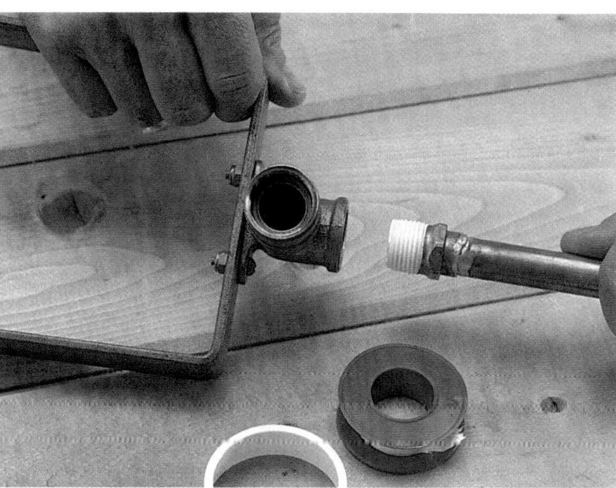

F. *Assemble the stand. Connect the stand pipe to one end of the shower ell and a garden hose connector to the other.*

Cobblestone Fountain

A cobblestone fountain, typically set flush with a paved garden path or surrounding grass, is attractive when the water isn't running, and delightful when it is. The cobblestone surface could be cut stone or smooth river rock, depending on your taste and what's available.

I loved building this fountain. In one afternoon, with one wheelbarrow-load of ordinary materials, I transformed a boring corner into a special place in the garden. And anyone can do it—the construction is simple and the materials are inexpensive.

You can use something as simple as a five-gallon bucket for the basin. In fact, any watertight plastic vessel at least 12" in diameter and 15" deep will work. To protect children and animals, you need to cover the opening of the basin with a sturdy grate. I used 9-gauge ¾" expanded metal mesh, which is available at some building centers or at any steel yard.

To eliminate weeds and help keep debris out of the basin, cover the excavated area with landscape fabric.

Set the pump on a brick to keep it above the floor of the basin and out of the residue that will collect there. For extra protection, you could put the pump in a clay pot, and then fill the pot with lava rocks that will filter debris.

The illustration at right shows dimensions that worked for the fountain I built, but you can adapt them as necessary to suit your location.

If you want to build a cobblestone fountain in an area not currently served by a GFCI outlet, install one near the proposed fountain location (page 108).

TOOLS & MATERIALS

- Shovel
- Tape measure
- Level
- Bolt cutters
- Metal file
- Hand tamp
- Plastic bucket or tub
- Sand
- Gravel
- Bricks (2)
- Submersible pump with telescoping delivery pipe
- Landscape fabric
- 9-gauge ¾" expanded metal mesh, 30" × 36"
- 6" paving stones, (approximately 35)
- Plants and decorative stones, as desired

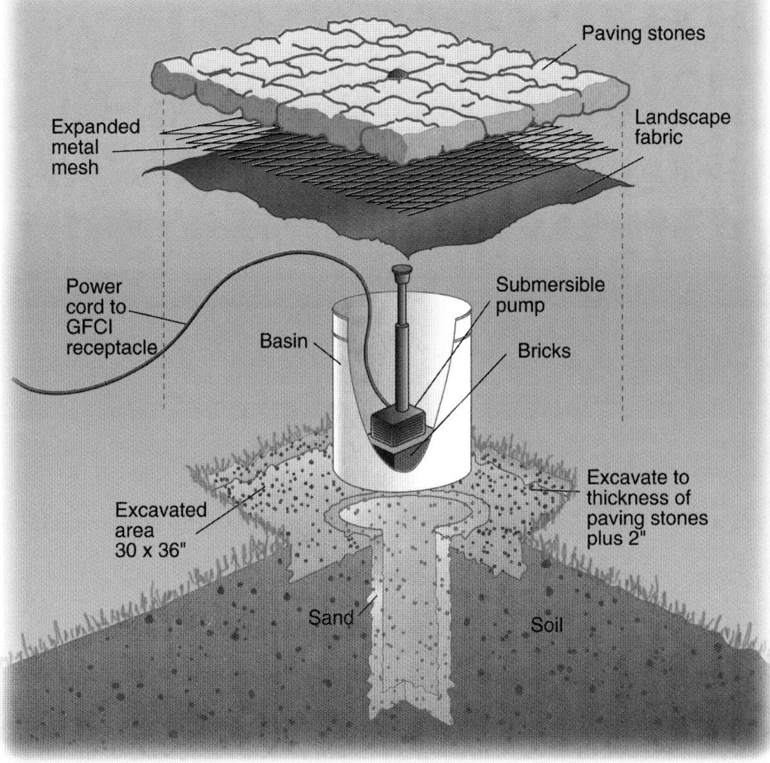

HOW TO BUILD A COBBLESTONE FOUNTAIN

Step A: Dig the Hole & Test Fit the Basin

1. Begin digging a hole 2" to 3" wider than the diameter of the bucket or tub you selected for the basin of the fountain. Keep the edges of the hole fairly straight, and the bottom fairly level.

2. Measure the height of the basin, add the height of the paving stones you've chosen, and then add 4" to this total. When the hole is approximately as deep as this combined measurement, test fit the basin and check it with a level. Remove dirt from the hole until the basin is as close as possible to level.

Step B: Dig the Paving Area

1. Cut out the grass or soil in a 30" × 36" rectangle surrounding the hole. To bring the surface of the fountain to ground level, dig this area 2" deeper than the height of the paving stones.

A. *Dig a hole approximately as deep as the combined height of the basin and the paving stones plus 4".*

B. *Cut out a 30" × 36" rectangle surrounding the hole, digging 2" deeper than the height of the paving stones.*

C. *Add a layer of gravel and then sand, tamping and adding sand until the top of the basin is level with the paving area.*

D. *Place the pump in the bucket, centered on the bricks. Position the electrical cord to run up and out of the hole.*

TIP

In the winter, you'll need to drain the fountain and remove the pump for storage. To empty the basin, remove the paving stones and the grate, and then place a small bucket under the spray, positioned to catch the water.

When the water level is as low as possible, remove the pump. Bail out whatever water remains, replace the grate and cover the fountain area with a tarp or sheet of heavy plastic.

2. Spread sand over the paving area, and then dampen and tamp the sand. Continue adding and tamping the sand until you've created a level 2" layer over the entire area.

Step C: Position the Basin

1. Add about 3" of gravel to the hole, and then add a 3" layer of sand. Dampen and tamp the sand; then test fit the basin again. Adjust until the top of the basin is level with the prepared paving area.

2. Fill the edges of the hole with gravel and/or sand to hold the basin firmly in place.

Step D: Install the Pump & the Grate

1. Clean out any sand or dirt, and then put two clean bricks on the bottom of the basin. Center the pump on top of the bricks; then extend the electrical cord up over the edge of the basin and out to the nearest GFCI receptacle.

2. Lay landscape fabric over the paving area. Extend the fabric over the edges of the basin by 5" or 6", and then trim it to shape.

Step E: Fill the Basin & Adjust the Flow Valve

Fill the basin with water. Turn on the pump and adjust the flow valve, following manufacturer's instructions. Adjust and test until the bubbling effect or spray appeals to you. (Keep in mind that the fountain's basic dimensions will be somewhat different when the paving stones are in place.)

Step F: Add the Paving Stones

1. Place the grate over the paving area, making sure the water delivery tube fits cleanly through an opening in the grate. If necessary, use bolt cutters and a metal file to enlarge the opening.

E. *Fill the basin with water and adjust the flow valve on the pump to create a pleasing effect.*

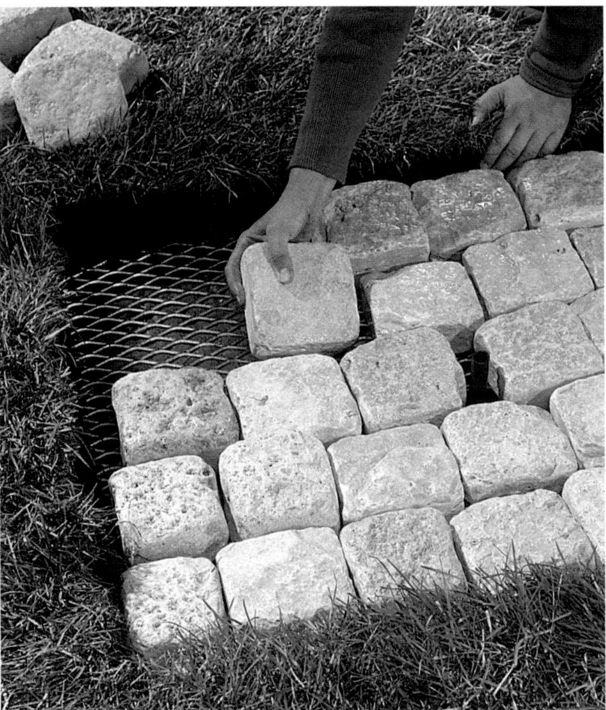

F. *Position the grate, and then set the paving stones in place. Be sure to leave space for water to recirculate between stones.*

2. Put the paving stones in place, setting them in evenly-spaced rows. Be sure to leave an area open around the water delivery pipe so the water has room to bubble up around the stones and then return to the basin.

Step G: Camouflage the Pump's Electrical Cord

Place plants and stones at the edge of the fountain to disguise the electrical cord as it exits the basin and runs toward the nearest GFCI receptacle.

VARIATION: PAVER OPTIONS

You can pave the fountain area with river stones, overlapping them in a fish-scale pattern.

You can even pave the fountain floor with a collection of colorful pebbles if you cover the grate with a second layer of landscape fabric to keep the pebbles from falling into the basin.

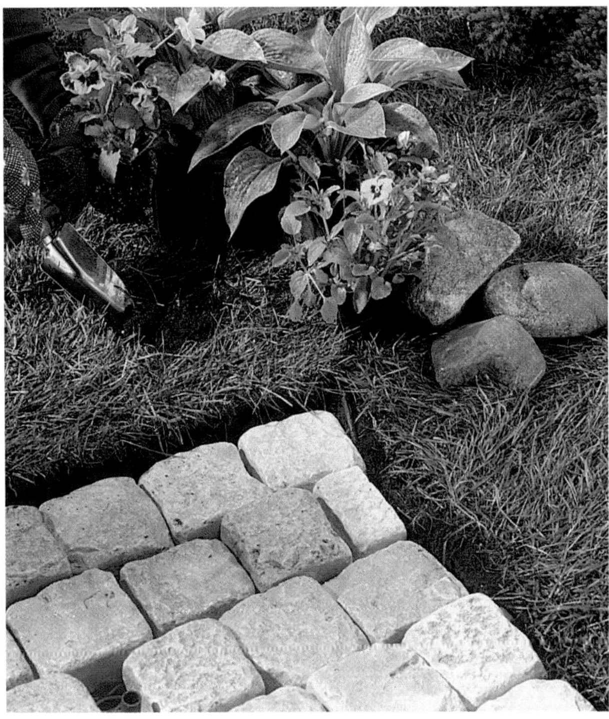

G. *Arrange plants and stones to disguise the electrical cord as it runs to the nearest GFCI receptacle.*

Hypertufa Birdbath

Birds add color, movement, and music to a garden. As if that's not enough to make them welcome guests, some species eat their weight in mosquitoes, grubs, and insects daily. The single most important thing you can do to attract birds is to provide a source of water, a fact that puts a birdbath near the top of my list of necessary garden ornaments.

I absolutely love this birdbath. It's sturdy, inexpensive, and easy to build, and its classic lines only improve with age. If you place it in a shady spot and encourage patches of moss to develop (page 53), it will blend into the landscape as if it's been part of your garden for decades.

It's made from hypertufa—a mixture of portland cement, peat moss, and sand or perlite. Working with hypertufa reminds me of childhood—it's like making mud pies, except that it dries into an attractive substance that holds its shape and stands up to years of use. For general instructions on working with hypertufa, see page 102. For this birdbath, use Recipe #2, which creates a watertight formula.

Since I frequently clean my birdbath, it's designed in sections that are easy to take apart. When it's assembled, the sections are held in place by interlocking pieces of PVC pipe that keep it from being toppled by strong winds or aggressive creatures.

To help attract birds to your birdbath, keep it clean, refill it with fresh water regularly, and place stones or branches in it to provide footing for your guests.

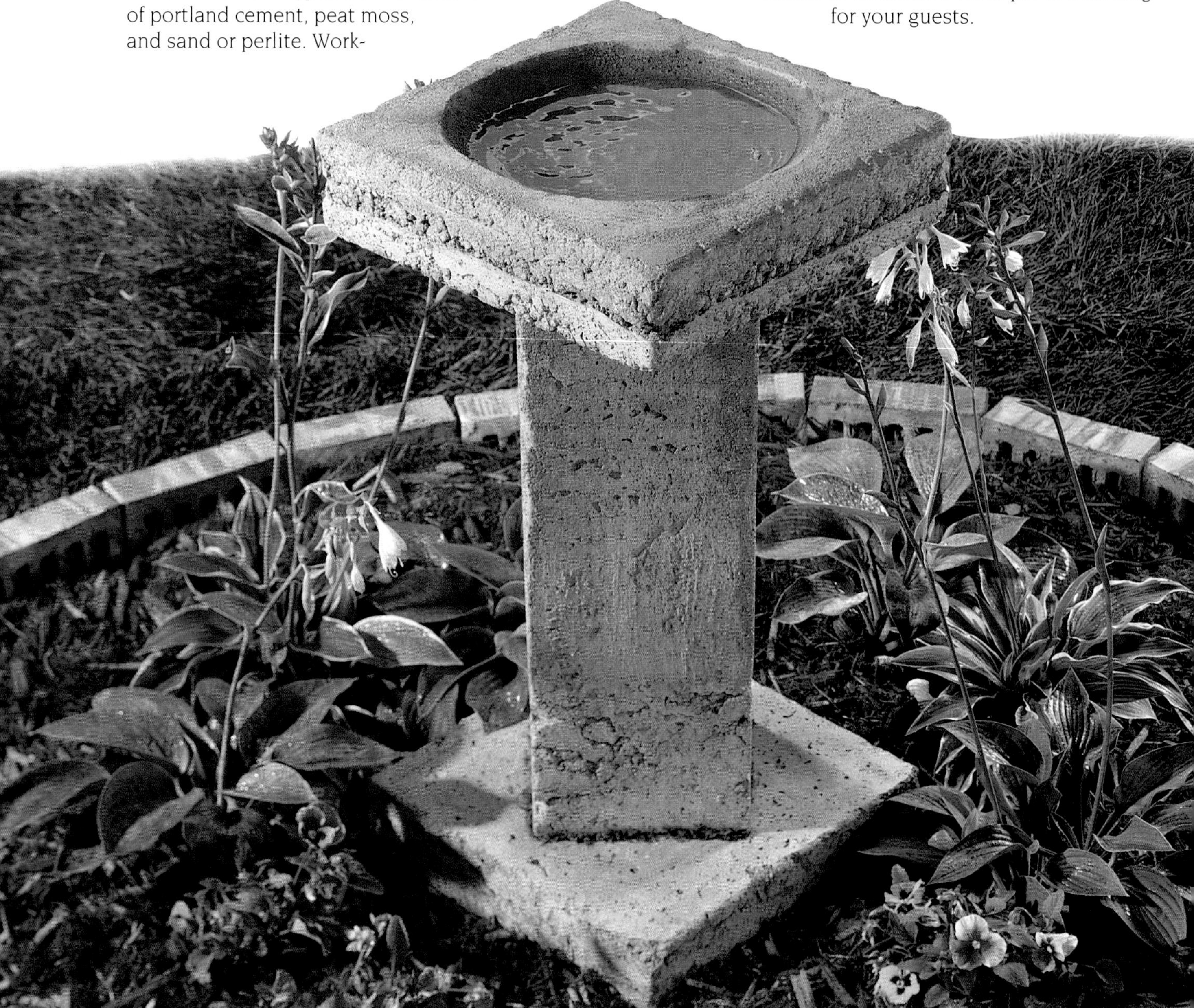

TOOLS & MATERIALS

- Tape measure
- Straightedge
- Jig saw
- Drill
- Hacksaw
- Hoe
- Trowel
- 2" polystyrene insulation board
- Gaffer's tape
- 3" deck screws
- Gloves
- Scrap of 2" PVC pipe, at least 6"
- 2" PVC pipe caps (4)
- Portland cement
- Peat moss
- Sand
- Scrap 2 × 4
- Shallow plastic bowl
- Vegetable oil

HOW TO BUILD A HYPERTUFA BIRDBATH

Step A: Build the Forms

1. Following the cutting list (below, right) measure and mark dimensions for the forms onto polystyrene insulation. Cut out the pieces, using a jig saw.

2. Construct the forms, supporting the joints with gaffer's tape (see page 103), then securing them with deck screws. The goal is to create forms for a 15" × 15" × 3½" base, a 15" × 15" × 3½" basin, and a 7¾" × 7¾" × 22" pedestal.

The mass of the pedestal piece creates quite a bit

A. *Build forms, using polystyrene insulation board, gaffer's tape, and deck screws.*

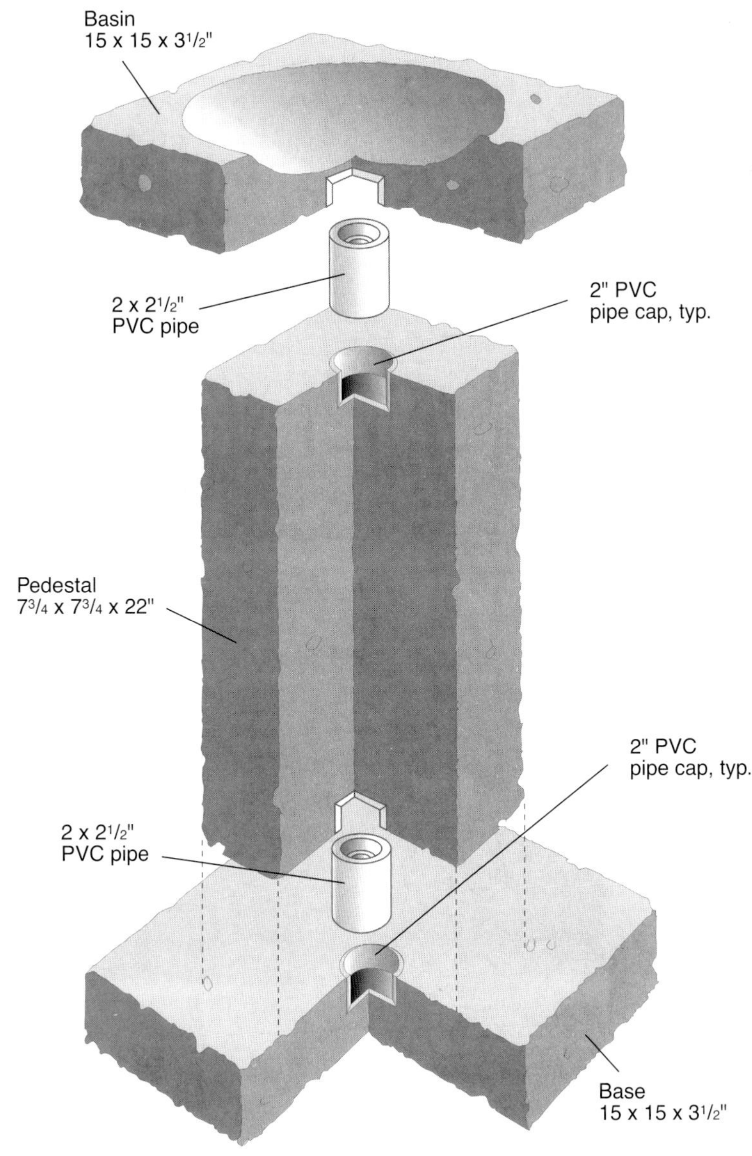

CUTTING LIST

Pedestal form	Basin & Base forms
7¾" × 22" (2)	15" × 5½" (4)
11¾" × 22" (2)	19" × 5½" (4)
11¾" × 11¾" (1)	15" × 15" (2)

of pressure against the walls of the form when the hypertufa is wet, so you may want to screw together a 1 × 2 collar to support the form, as shown in Photo C. Or, you could use strap clamps to reinforce the forms, if necessary .

Step B: Pour the Base

1. Mix the hypertufa, using Recipe #2 (see page 102 for recipe and instructions).

2. Mark the center of the form, and then center a pipe cap exactly over the mark, open side down. Pack hypertufa into the form, and tamp it down, using a short piece of 2 × 4. Continue packing and tamping until the hypertufa is level with the top of the form.

3. Rap the surface with the 2 × 4 to eliminate air bubbles. Smooth the surface, using a trowel. Cover the piece with plastic and allow it to cure.

Step C: Pour the Pedestal

1. Mark the exact center of the bottom of the pedestal form, and then place the open end of a PVC pipe cap on the form, centered over the mark.

2. Pack hypertufa into the form until it's nearly level with the top. Insert a PVC pipe cap at the center of the form, open side up, so its top edge is flush with the top of the form. Tamp and smooth as directed in #3 of Step B. Cover the piece with plastic and allow it to cure.

Step D: Pour the Basin

1. Mark the center on the bottom of the form, and press the open end of a PVC pipe cap into the form, centered over that mark.

2. Pack the hypertufa into the form in a layer about 2" thick.

3. Coat a shallow, gently sloped plastic bowl with vegetable oil, and then press it into the hypertufa, forming the depression of the basin. Continue packing and tamping the hypertufa around the bowl until you've created a smooth, even surface that's level with the top of the form. When the hypertufa is set, remove the bowl, cover the basin with plastic, and let it cure.

Step E: Construct the Birdbath

1. After the pieces have dried for 48 hours, disassemble the forms and remove the pieces of the birdbath. If you like a weathered look, now's the time to distress the pieces. Using a hammer and chisel, knock off corners and remove any sharp edges (see page 103).

2. Set the pieces outside, cover them with a tarp,

***B.** Place the open end of a PVC pipe cap over the exact center of the base form. Pack and tamp hypertufa into the form, making sure the end cap stays in place. Add hypertufa until it reaches the top of the form.*

***C.** Place a PVC pipe cap over the center of the bottom of the pedestal form, and then pack hypertufa into the form. Embed a PVC pipe cap at the top of the pedestal, centered within the form.*

TIP: ATTRACTING BIRDS TO YOUR GARDEN

If you want to attract birds to your garden, remember that they have much the same physical needs as humans: water, shelter, and food. Include garden features that will satisfy these needs—a birdbath, water garden, or fountain for water; trees, shrubs, and birdhouses for shelter; feeders or edible plants for food.

You can encourage birds to make a home in your garden by choosing plants that appeal to them. Hummingbirds are drawn to bright flowers, especially red and violet annuals. Other birds are attracted by sunflowers, marigolds, asters, and other flowers that produce lots of seeds, especially if you let the plants go to seed rather than deadheading them.

Birds are attracted to water at ground level, but that puts them in a vulnerable position when predators approach. Place water basins two to three feet above ground and close enough to shrubs or trees that birds have a place to flee if necessary—but not so close that predators can hide in them.

Clean your birdbath thoroughly every few days: Remove algae and bird droppings, and wash the basin with a solution of vinegar and water.

and let them cure for several weeks. Every few days, rinse the pieces with water to remove some of the alkaline residue from the hypertufa.

3. After several weeks, move the pieces back indoors and protect them from moisture. When you're sure the hypertufa is completely dry, paint a coat of good quality masonry sealer onto the depression of the basin.

4. Cut two 2½" pieces of 2" PVC pipe, using a hacksaw. Make sure the cuts are square.

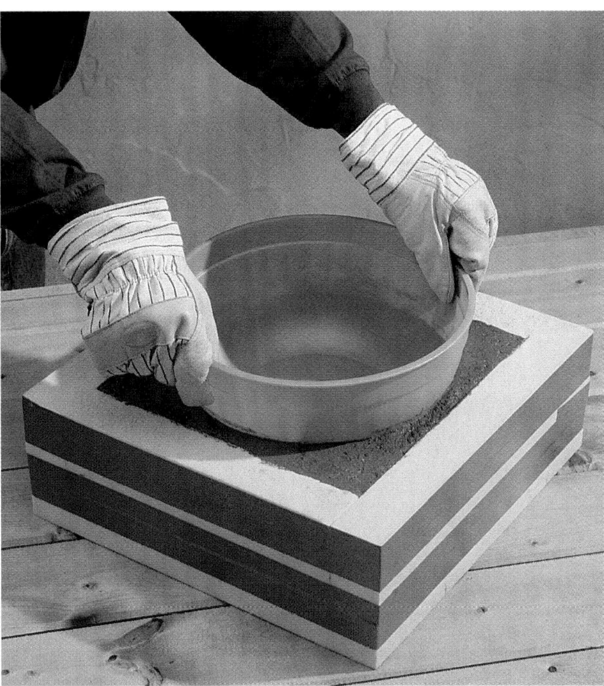

D. *Place a PVC pipe cap at the exact center of the basin form, and then pack a layer of hypertufa into the form. Use an oiled plastic bowl to create a depression in the basin.*

5. Position the base, and then insert one 2½" piece of pipe into the pipe cap at the center of the base. Align the pieces and connect the PVC pipe to the cap embedded in the pedestal.

6. Insert the other 2½" piece of pipe in the cap at the bottom of the basin. Align this pipe with the cap on the top of the pedestal, joining the pieces.

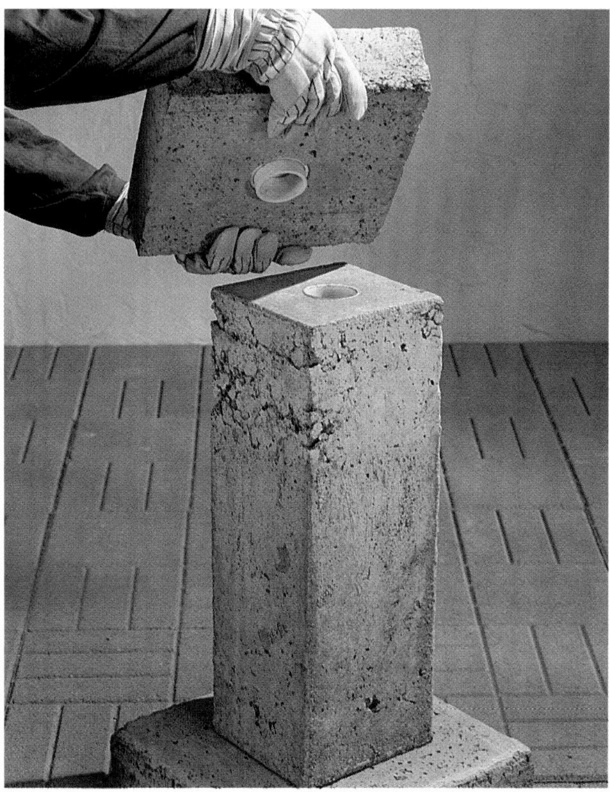

E. *Insert a 2½" piece of PVC pipe into the cap at the center of the base and connect it to the pipe cap in the bottom of the pedestal. Insert another 2½" piece of PVC pipe into the cap in the basin and connect it to the cap in the pedestal.*

Roses
Coleus

Accent Pieces

Accent pieces are the details—the grace notes—of a garden. These little flourishes transform your garden from a collection of random elements into a cohesive atmosphere of your own choosing. They also reinforce the impression that the person who tends this garden loves his or her work, down to the smallest detail.

I'm not suggesting that attractive plant markers (page 32) will make your flowers bloom more abundantly or that innovative hose guards (page 33) will protect your borders more vigilantly than plain ones, but I can assure you they'll make you and your visitors smile. And like me, you may take special pleasure in strolling along a path of stepping stones you created yourself (page 34) or in watching a delighted child hopscotch from one to the next. Brightly painted birdhouses (page 40) may not attract more birds, but they will attract more attention.

Most of the projects in this chapter include variations and suggestions for ways to adapt the basic ideas to suit your own tastes and style. By virtue of their small scale, accent pieces offer inexpensive, low-risk opportunities to experiment with unusual materials and new ideas. Accent pieces also make terrific gifts for other gardeners.

IN THIS CHAPTER:

Stakes, Markers, & Hose Guards

Marking and supporting plants remind me of housekeeping—not particularly thrilling, but necessary. However, even maintenance tasks can be fun if you take a lighthearted approach. With a handful of inexpensive materials and a couple of hours, you can build special stakes, markers, and hose guards that add splashes of color or touches of whimsy as they help you maintain your garden.

The plant stakes shown here are easy to make, but the soldering may take a bit of practice. You have to work quickly to avoid reheating, and thereby softening, the previous joints.

Plant markers are traditionally used to identify plants; the generous size of these markers also gives you a handy place to keep notes about a plant's care requirements. You can use permanent markers to add color-coded symbols to the back of each marker, identifying plants that require staking, indicating the best pruning time, and noting any special fertilization needs.

TOOLS & MATERIALS

- Tape measure
- Tubing cutter
- Diagonal pliers
- Propane torch
- Pliers
- Drill
- Hacksaw
- Hand maul
- 1/4" flexible copper tubing
- 6-gauge copper wire
- 12-gauge copper wire
- 1/2" copper pipe (4")
- Flux
- Solder
- 1 1/2" glass marble
- 1" glass marble
- 1/2" glass marble
- 10-gauge plastic-coated wire (3 ft.)
- #3 rebar (30")

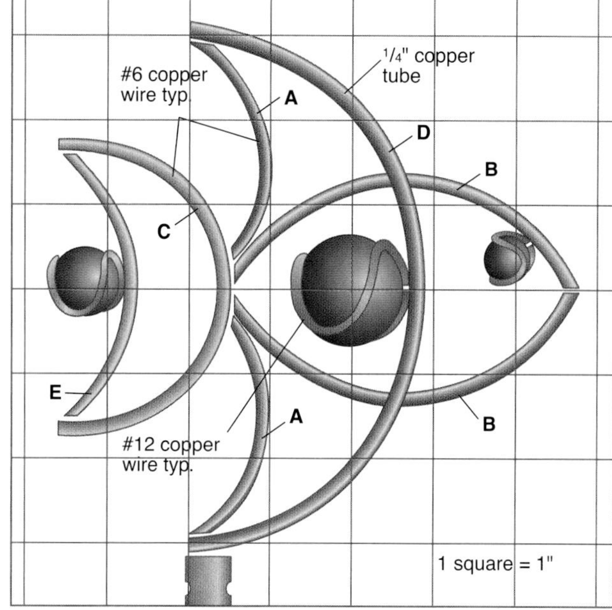

HOW TO MAKE GARDEN STAKES

Step A: Create the Outline

1. Using the grid system or a photocopier, enlarge the pattern at right, and tack it to a work surface.

2. Use a tubing cutter to cut a piece of 1/4" copper tubing to the approximate length of the front arc of the fish's fin. Use diagonal pliers to cut a piece of 6-gauge copper wire to the approximate length of each remaining piece of the fish. Place the copper over the pattern, bend each piece to match the pattern line it represents, and then cut the pieces to fit.

3. Layer the pieces together to form the design. Start with the body of the fish. Add the two arcs that form the back of the fin, and then the front arc of the fin. Finally, position the tail pieces.

4. On a heat-resistant surface, solder the joints (see page 100). Begin by joining the back arcs of the fin (A) and the main pieces of the body (B). Add the first piece of the tail (C). Let these joints cool until they're rigid and have lost their shine.

5. Add the front arc of the fin (D), soldering it only to the fish body and the top fin joint. Solder the remaining piece of the tail (E) in place. Let the joints cool completely.

Step B: Add the Embellishments & the Stem

1. Cut a 4" piece of 1/2" copper pipe. About 1" from one end, drill a hole through each side of the pipe. Position the pipe at the lower fin joint of the fish. Solder the joint closed, connecting the fish to the pipe in the process.

2. Cut three pieces of #12 copper wire: 6 3/4", 5 1/2",

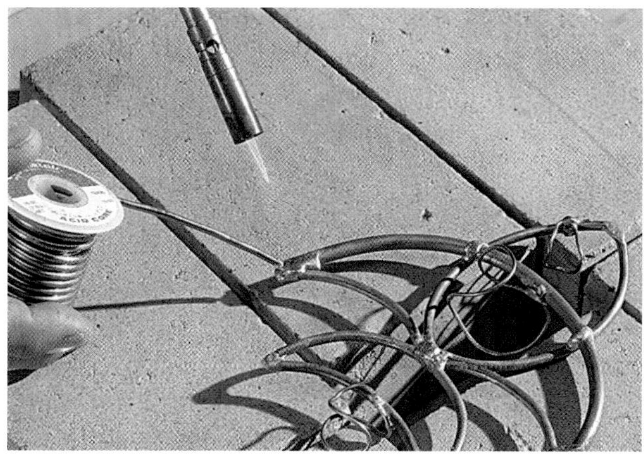

A. *Cut copper tubing and shape it to match the pattern. Layer the pieces together, and then solder the joints.*

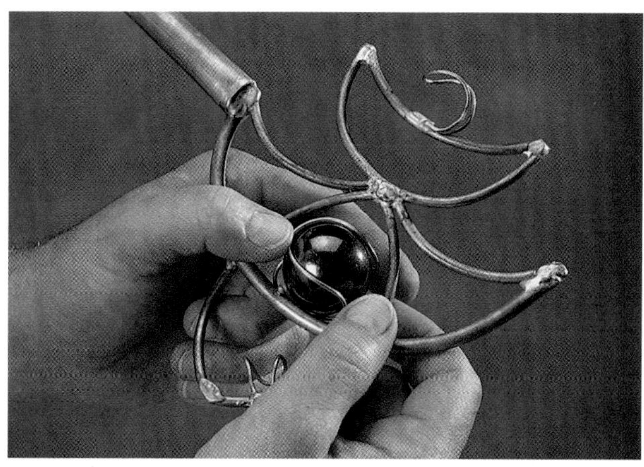

B. *Form wire circles and solder them into position. Bend the circles into loops to support the marbles.*

and 3¾". Form each piece into a circle, and then solder the circles in place, following the diagram on page 31. Let the solder cool completely.

3. Fold each wire circle into a loop, put a marble in its center, and shape the wire to hold the marble in place.

Step C: Install the Stake

1. Cut a 30" piece of rebar, using a hacksaw. With a hand maul, drive the rebar into the garden soil about 12". Set the fish ornament over the rebar.

2. Thread a 3-ft. piece of plastic coated wire through the holes at the top of the copper pipe. Bend each half of the wire back around the pipe, and then use pliers to make a 1" hook at each end. Surround the plant with the wires, and hook them together to support heavy stems.

C. *Thread plastic-coated wire through the stem of the ornament, and wrap it back around the stem. Form a hook at each end; loop the hooks together to support the plant.*

TOOLS & MATERIALS

- Straightedge
- Awl
- Mallet
- Aviation snips
- Drill
- Kitchen tongs
- Sheet of thin copper
- 100-grit sandpaper
- Fine steel wool
- Spray acrylic sealer
- ¾" copper pipe (10")
- 8-gauge galvanized wire
- Raffia or natural twine
- Permanent marker
- Wood backer

HOW TO MAKE GARDEN MARKERS

Step A: Create the Designs

1. Draw the outline for the tags on a sheet of copper, using a pencil. Draw a second line, repeating the shape, ¼" to ½" inside the outline.

2. Mark a hanging hole about ⅛" from the top edge of each tag and centered within the design. Place the copper over a smooth piece of wood, and then use an awl and a mallet to punch the hanging hole.

3. Punch decorative holes about ⅛" apart around the inside line of each tag.

4. Cut out the design along the traced outline, using aviation snips. Trim off sharp points, if necessary. Remove any rough edges by lightly sanding the edges of the tags with 100-grit sandpaper.

5. Hold each tag over a flame, such as the burner of a gas range, using tongs. Move the tag randomly

A. *Mark outlines onto copper sheet; mark hanging holes, and use an awl and a mallet to punch a design.*

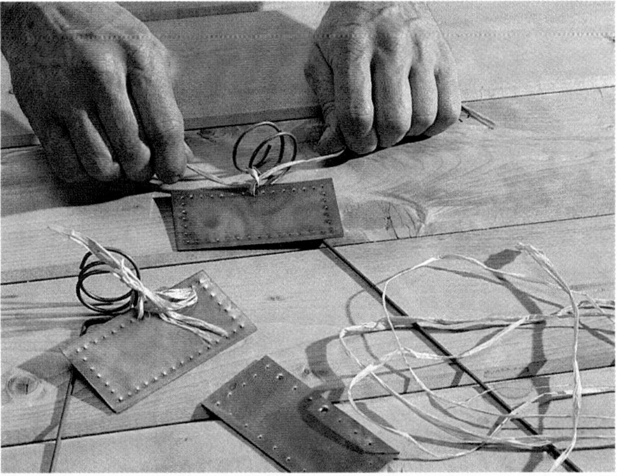

B. *Sand the edges of the tags, oxidize the surface of each, then spray with acrylic sealer. Thread raffia through the hanging hole and loop it onto a stake made from 8-gauge galvanized wire.*

through the flame to produce color changes, checking it occasionally. Let the tags cool.

6. Lightly rub the tags with fine steel wool to remove any fingerprints; wipe clean. Spray each tag with acrylic sealer and let it dry.

7. Use a permanent marker to write a plant name on each tag.

Step B: Make the Stakes & Hang the Tags

1. To create a bending jig, drill a hole through a piece of 3/4" copper pipe, and clamp the pipe in a vise. For each stake, cut a 21" piece of 8-gauge galvanized wire, using aviation snips. Insert one end of the wire into the hole in the pipe, and wrap the wire twice around the pipe. Snip off the wire at the hole and remove the stake.

2. Push the stake about 6" into the garden soil. Thread a 3" piece of raffia through the tag, and then through the loop of the stake, and tie it securely.

TOOLS & MATERIALS

- Paintbrush
- Hand maul
- Drill
- Wood deck post finials
- Exterior paint or stain or wood sealer
- Garden stakes

HOW TO MAKE HOSE GUARDS

Install Stakes & Add Finials

1. Stain and seal deck post finials, or paint them with two coats of exterior paint, depending on the finish you prefer. Let them dry thoroughly.

2. Position the finials to guide the hose around your planting beds rather than through them. Mark their locations, and drive a garden stake flush with the soil at each marked spot, using a hand maul. Drill a pilot hole and screw a finial into each stake.

Drive garden stakes flush with the soil, and then screw one finial into each stake.

VARIATION: DRAIN TILE HOSE GUARDS

You can make simple but attractive hose guards from ordinary drain tile. Place the tiles around the edges of a border, positioning them to keep the hose from being dragged across the planting area. Mark these positions.

At each mark, dig a hole the same diameter as the drain tile and approximately 6" deep. Set a drain tile into each hole and adjust until the tile's level.

Add a 2½" layer of pea gravel, and then fill the drain tile with potting soil and add plants.

Dig a 6"-deep hole for each drain tile. Set the drain tile in place and adjust until it's level. Add pea gravel and potting soil; plant as desired.

Stepping Stones

In some gardens, stepping stone paths beckon, virtually begging to be followed. Handmade stones add a unique, personal touch to a garden—you can even inscribe them to commemorate special days, such as birthdays or anniversaries.

This is a great project to share with children—there's almost no way to go wrong and you can use a nearly infinite variety of materials, depending on the ages and interests of the children. There are many stepping-stone kits on the market, but you don't need one—the materials are readily available.

To form stepping stones, use quick-setting concrete mix. I usually estimate one 40-lb. bag of mix for each 18"-square stone. This mix is caustic: Wear a dust mask and gloves when using it.

Experiment with textures, patterns, and shapes. If you don't like a pattern, smooth the surface and start again. Remember, though, that you must work fairly quickly—quick-setting concrete sets up within 30 minutes. To slow the process, you can lightly mist the surface with water after "erasing" a pattern.

In addition to the decorative techniques described on the next page, you can make gorgeous accent stones from pieces of broken china or pottery. You can buy broken bits of china at craft stores, but it's less expensive to buy old dishes at garage sales or flea markets and break them yourself. Place the dishes in a heavy paper bag and then tap the bag with a rubber mallet. Wear safety goggles and heavy gloves when handling broken pieces, and file any sharp edges with a masonry file.

TOOLS & MATERIALS

- Shovel
- Hand tamp
- Containers to be used as molds
- Petroleum jelly
- Gloves
- Dust mask
- Quick-setting concrete mix
- Bucket
- Mason's trowel
- Embellishments, as desired
- Compactible gravel

HOW TO BUILD STEPPING STONES

Step A: Prepare the Molds & Pour the Concrete

1. Select molds for the stepping stones. Use aluminum pie plates, plastic plant saucers or large plastic lids, plywood forms or shallow boxes. Select molds deep enough (1½" to 2") and large enough (12" to 18") to make stones that can bear weight and comfortably accommodate an adult's foot.

2. Fill the molds with dry concrete mix to estimate the amount necessary. Following manufacturer's instructions, mix water, concrete dye if desired, and the concrete mix. Check a handful—it should hold its shape when squeezed, something like cookie dough. If necessary, add water and mix again.

3. Coat the molds with petroleum jelly, covering all the corners and edges.

4. Fill the forms with concrete. Smooth the surface with a mason's trowel, and then use a scrap 2 × 4 to skim off any excess water.

Step B: Embellish the Surface

1. Decorate the stones as desired.

Stamping Technique: Let the concrete dry for 10 to 15 minutes. While it's still damp, press ornaments firmly onto the surface, and then remove them. You can use a variety of natural ornaments such as leaves, twigs, small evergreen branches, shells, or stones. Or, you can use rubber stamps, available at craft stores.

Embedding Technique: Let the concrete dry for 10 minutes. Press ornaments into the surface, partially submerging them. Make sure the ornaments are firmly settled into the cement.

2. Let the stones cure several hours or overnight. Remove them from the molds.

Step C: Install the Stepping Stones

1. Cut out the turf and dig out 3½" to 4" of soil, following the shape of the stones.

2. Add a 2" layer of compactible gravel and tamp it thoroughly. Test-fit each stone, adjusting the gravel layer until the stone is level and stable.

A. *Select molds; coat them with petroleum jelly. Mix quick-setting concrete and fill the molds. Skim off excess water.*

B. *Decorate the stones with stamped designs or embedded ornaments. Let the stepping stones harden thoroughly.*

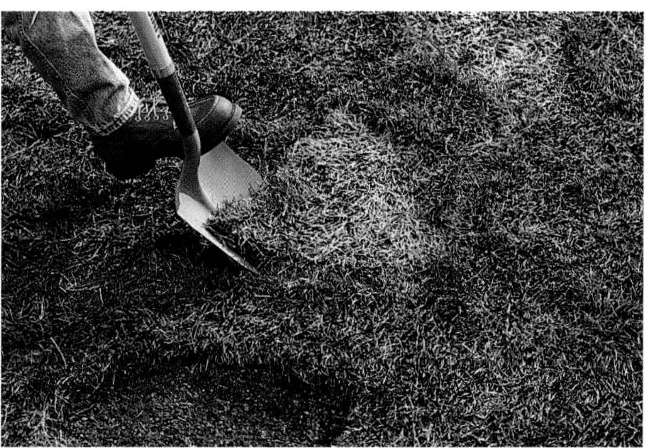

C. *Cut out the turf and remove 3½" to 4" of soil. Add a layer of compactible gravel, and then set each stone in place. Adjust until each stone is level and stable.*

Garden Lantern

Candles instantly create a romantic atmosphere, perhaps because they cast a soft, warm glow that's flattering to both people and places. Low-voltage lights illuminate many gardens, but even the most sophisticated lighting systems can't duplicate the mood that candles create. Some times and circumstances call for candlelight, even in the garden.

By combining a handful of copper plumbing supplies (perhaps left over from another copper project in this book) and a few other inexpensive materials, you can create a garden lantern that enhances your garden by day as well as by night. This easy-to-assemble design makes ingenious use of common materials. Reshaped copper pipe straps form a support system for the top and bottom of the lantern; a ring of silicone caulk provides a buffer to keep the hurricane globe from tipping or rattling; a brass machine screw secures the candle to the frame; a threaded brass rod connects the frame to the hanging arch.

Before you go shopping for a candle or hurricane globe, check the dimensions in the diagram on page 37. Be sure the globe you select is proportional to the lantern and leaves enough clearance for you to light the candle with a long match.

Note: *Although the sturdy framework and hurricane globe of this lantern shelter the candle, as with any open flame, it should not be left unattended while burning.*

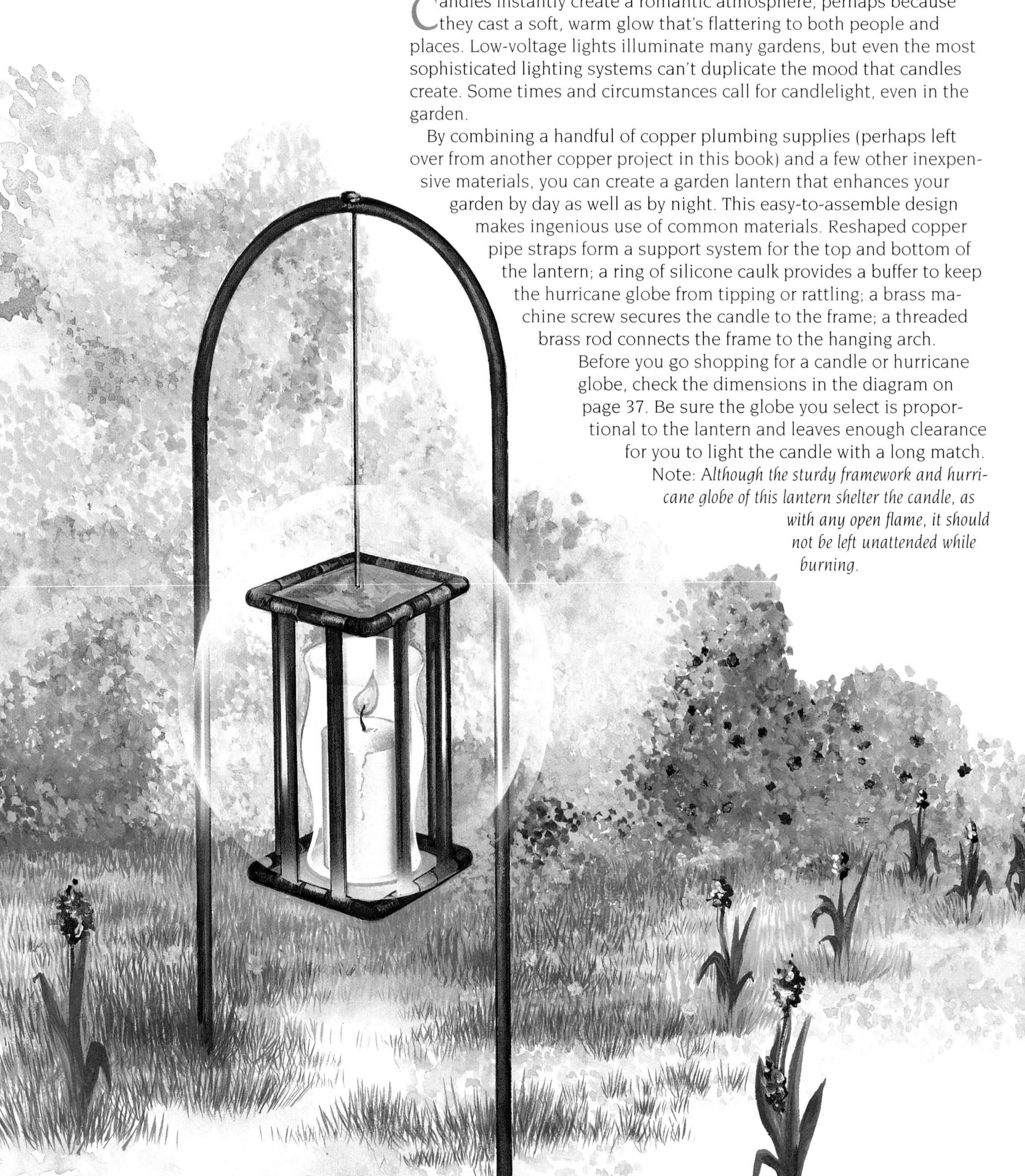

TOOLS & MATERIALS

- Tape measure
- Tubing cutter
- Propane torch
- Flux brush
- Aviation snips
- Drill
- Hand maul
- ½" copper pipe (10 ft.)
- ½" copper 90° elbows (8)
- ½" copper tees (16)
- Gaffer's tape
- Emery cloth
- Flux
- Sheet of thin copper, at least 16" square
- ½" copper pipe straps (8)
- #6-32 × ⅜" brass machine screws (8)
- #6-32 brass machine screw nuts (9)
- #6-32 × 2½" machine screw
- Silicone caulk
- Petroleum jelly
- ⅛" threaded brass rod, 11" long
- Nuts to fit threaded rod (3)
- Acorn nut to fit threaded rod
- ⅝" flexible copper tubing, 100" long
- Plywood, 20" × 20"
- #4 rebar, 30" long (2)
- Candle
- Hurricane globe

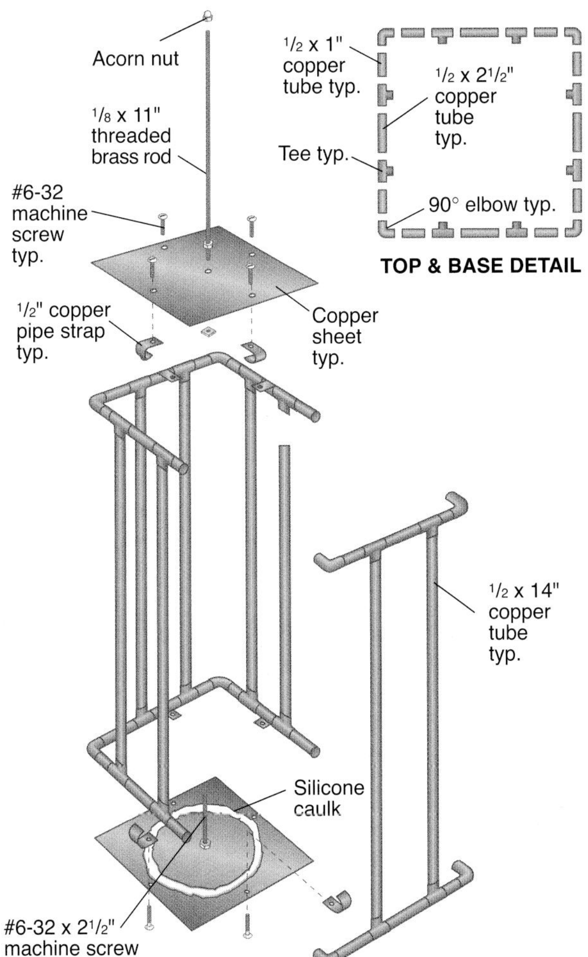

HOW TO BUILD A GARDEN LANTERN

Step A: Cut the Pipe & Construct the Frame

1. Measure and mark the copper pipe, following the cutting list shown below.

2. Cut the copper pipe, using a tubing cutter. Place the cutter over the pipe and tighten the handle until the pipe rests on both rollers and the cutting wheel is positioned over the the marked line. Turn the tubing cutter one rotation, so that the cutting wheel

A. *Connect copper pipes, elbows, and tees to form the base of the frame, and then add the legs and top.*

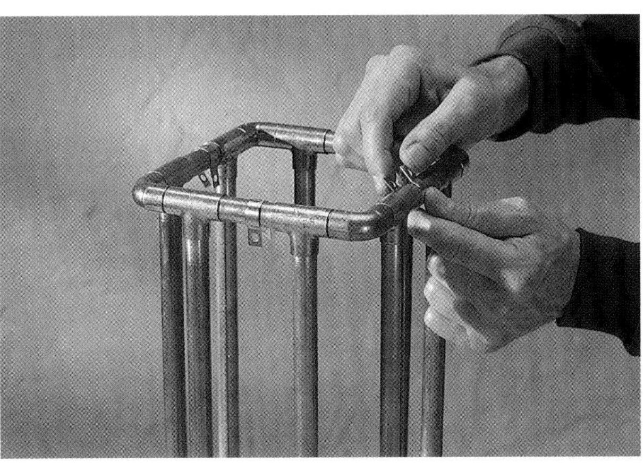

B. *Bend pipe straps around the sides of the frame, positioning them to support the covers on the base and top of the lantern.*

CUTTING LIST

½" Copper Pipe

Quantity	Length
8	14"
8	2½"
16	1"

scores a continuous straight line around the pipe. Rotate the cutter in the opposite direction, tightening the handle slightly after every two rotations until the cut is complete. Remove any sharp metal burrs from the inside edges of the cut pipe, using the reaming point on the tubing cutter or a round file.

3. Clean and flux the pipes, tees, and elbows (see page 100). Dry fit the pieces of the frame, top, and base, following the diagram on page 37. If you have

C. *Cut a piece of sheet copper for the base cover and secure it to the pipe straps, using machine screws and nuts. Add a circle of silicone caulk to buffer the lantern's globe.*

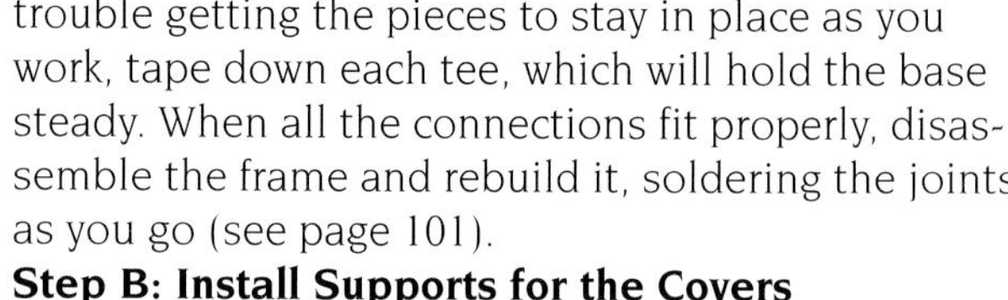

trouble getting the pieces to stay in place as you work, tape down each tee, which will hold the base steady. When all the connections fit properly, disassemble the frame and rebuild it, soldering the joints as you go (see page 101).

Step B: Install Supports for the Covers

1. Center one ½" copper pipe strap along each side of the top and each side of the bottom of the frame. Wrap one side of each strap around the pipe and extend the other end toward the center of the frame. Later, these extensions will support the base and top.

Step C: Add the Base Cover

1. Measure the inside dimensions of the base of the frame, and then mark and cut a sheet of copper to match, using aviation snips. Position the base so the straps support the edges, and mark the locations of the pipe strap holes. Drill a hole through the cover at each of these marks, as well as at the exact center of the cover.

2. Center the globe over the hole in the middle of the base, draw a pencil line just outside the lip, then remove the globe. To form a buffer for the globe, run a bead of silicone caulk around this circle, just inside the line. While the caulk sets up, apply petroleum jelly to the lip of the globe and use it to make an impression in the bead of caulk.

3. Working up from the bottom, attach the base cover to the frame, threading #6-32 × ⅜" machine screws through the pipe straps and the sheet of copper and securing them with machine screw nuts.

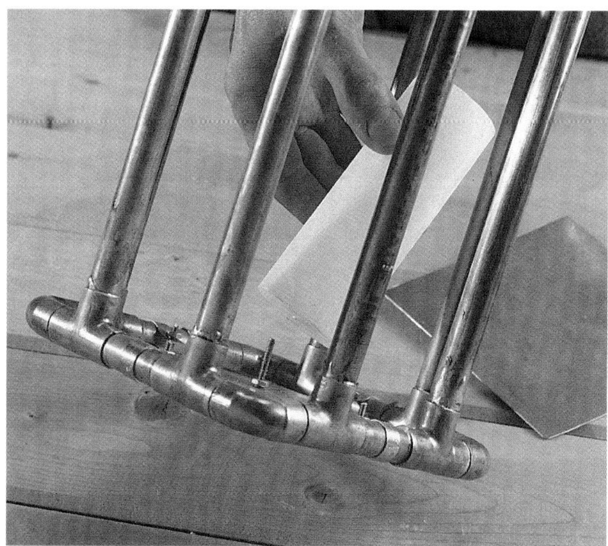

D. *Run a 2½" machine screw through the center of the base cover and secure it with a nut. Thread a candle onto the screw, and then settle the hurricane globe into place.*

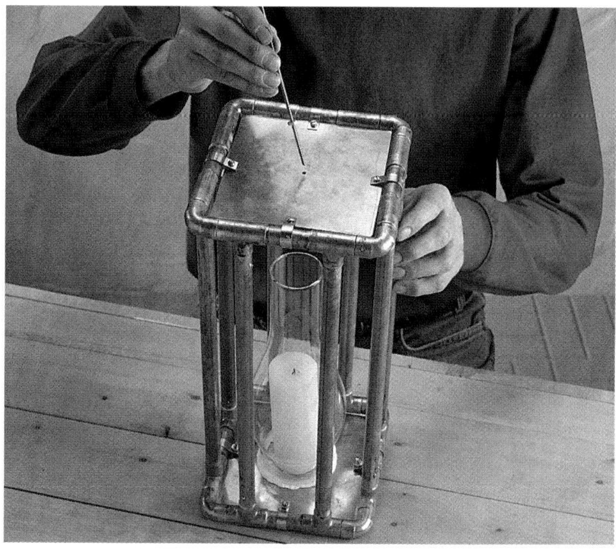

E. *Run a piece of threaded brass rod through the center of the top and secure it with one nut above and one below the sheet of copper.*

Step D: Position the Candle & Hurricane Globe

Run a #6-32 × 2½" machine screw through the hole in the center of the base cover and secure it with a nut. Thread the candle onto the screw, and then position the hurricane globe over the candle.

Step E: Install the Top Cover & Hanging Rod

1. Measure the inside dimensions of the top of the frame, and then mark a sheet of copper to match. Cut the sheet, using aviation snips. Position the top cover and mark the locations of the pipe strap holes. Drill a hole at each mark as well as at the exact center of the cover.

2. Working from the top down, secure the top cover to the frame, again using #6-32 × ⅜" machine screws and machine screw nuts.

3. Insert the threaded rod through the hole in the center of the top, and secure it with one nut below and one above.

Step F: Create the Arch & Hang the Lantern

1. Cut a 100" piece of ⅝" flexible copper tubing. Mark the center, and drill a ⅛" hole all the way through the tubing.

2. Cut a plywood circle 20" in diameter, mark it into quadrants, and clamp or screw it to a workbench. Line up the hole in the tubing with the marked top of the plywood circle, and bend the sides of the tubing down around the circle, forming a smooth arch.

3. Select a location and press the arch into the ground to mark the leg positions. At each mark, drive a 30" piece of #4 rebar about 18" into the ground.

4. Slide the legs of the arch over the rebar and press down to seat the copper firmly into the ground.

5. Screw a nut onto the hanging rod, and then insert the rod into the hole at the center of the arch. Thread an acorn nut onto the rod and tighten it.

F. *Add a nut to the top of the hanging rod; slide it through the hole in the supporting arch. Secure the rod with an acorn nut.*

VARIATION: ICE LUMINARIES

Gardens sometimes look forlorn in winter. When temperatures consistently remain below freezing, brighten and warm your garden with ice luminaries.

For each ice luminary, you need a plastic jar such as a mayonnaise or peanut butter jar, a handful of rocks, and a one-gallon bucket. Fill the jar with rocks, and place it in the center of the bucket. Add water to the bucket until it reaches the rim of the jar.

Set the bucket outside or in a freezer until the water freezes. Remove the rocks, and pour warm water into the jar. When the ice releases the jar, remove it.

Wrap the outside of the bucket with a warm, wet towel until it releases the ice. Remove the ice from the bucket. Place a candle in the center well and put the luminary in the garden.

These luminaries last for quite a while if temperatures stay below freezing. If the ice gets cloudy, spraying it with water will clear it.

Ice luminaries warm and brighten dark winter nights.

Birdhouse

Birds, like humans, go where they feel most welcome. They prefer gardens that offer fresh water, plentiful food, and comfortable shelter. In addition to birdbaths and feeders, birdhouses are an essential part of attracting birds to your garden.

I've found that many cavity-nesting birds are drawn to birdhouses about 4" square and about 8" tall. If you build the house so that one side pivots open, you can clean the house after nesting season or remove nests built by birds you don't want to encourage.

To build comfortable, long-lasting birdhouses, use 1 × 6 cedar or redwood lumber. The thickness of the lumber provides some insulation against both heat and cold, and the cedar or redwood, which is weather resistant, helps the house withstand the elements for several years. You can paint the outside of a birdhouse, but never the interior. Subdued colors such as brown, tan, and gray are good choices because they're pleasing to many types of birds.

Before you start building birdhouses, decide what species of birds you want to invite to your garden. The recommended diameter of the entrance hole and the height for mounting the birdhouse (see chart on page 42) depends on the species you're trying to attract.

Although the birdhouse shown below is designed to be hung, you can easily adapt the plans to build a birdhouse that can be mounted vertically or on a garden post (page 43).

TOOLS & MATERIALS

- Drill and 1/16" bit
- Spade bit sized for desired entrance hole
- Jig saw or circular saw
- Carpenter's square
- Cordless screwdriver
- 1 × 6 redwood or cedar
- 4d galvanized finish nails
- Exterior wood glue
- Shoulder hook
- Screw eyes (2)

A. *Trim diagonally across each corner, 1/2" from the corners.*

HOW TO BUILD A HANGING BIRDHOUSE

Note: *Cut all pieces from 1 × 6 cedar lumber. The actual measurements of dimensional lumber vary: Make sure the lumber you select measures 5 1/2" in width.*

Step A: Cut the Bottom & Sides of the House

1. Cut a 4" square for the bottom of the house. Trim diagonally across each corner, 1/2" from the corner, to allow for drainage.

2. Cut two 4" × 5 1/2" pieces for the sides of the house.

Step B: Cut the Front, Back, & Roof

1. Cut two 5 1/2" × 8 3/4" pieces, one for the front and one for the back of the house.

2. On each piece, mark a point 2 3/4" down from the top on each adjacent side. Draw lines from the center point down to these side points, then cut along these lines.

3. Cut one 5 1/2"× 6 1/2" piece and one 4 3/4" × 6 1/2" piece for the roof.

B. *Mark the center of the front, and then use a carpenter's square to mark the pitch of the roof. Cut along marked lines. Repeat for the back of the house.*

Step C: Drill the Entrance Hole & Score Grip Lines

1. Mark a point on the front piece, 6 3/4" from the lower edge, centering the mark from side to side. Place the tip of a spade bit on the marked point and drill an entrance hole. Begin at low speed, and gradually increase the speed as the bit enters the wood.

2. Use a wood screw or an awl to make several deep horizontal scratches on the inside of the front piece, starting 1" below the entrance hole. These grip lines help young birds hold on as they climb up to the entrance hole.

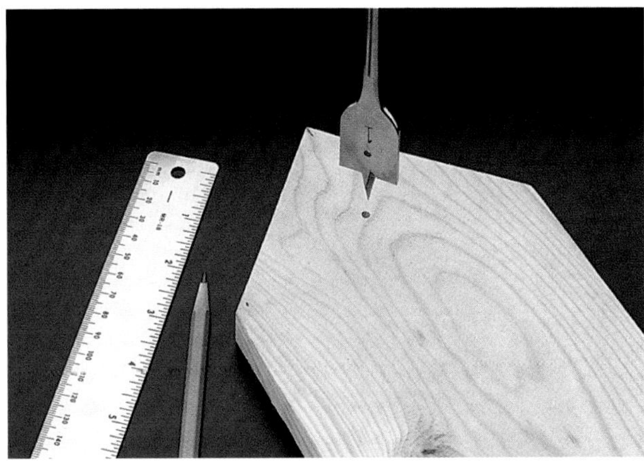

C. *Center a mark 6 3/4" from the lower edge. Drill the entrance hole, using a spade bit.*

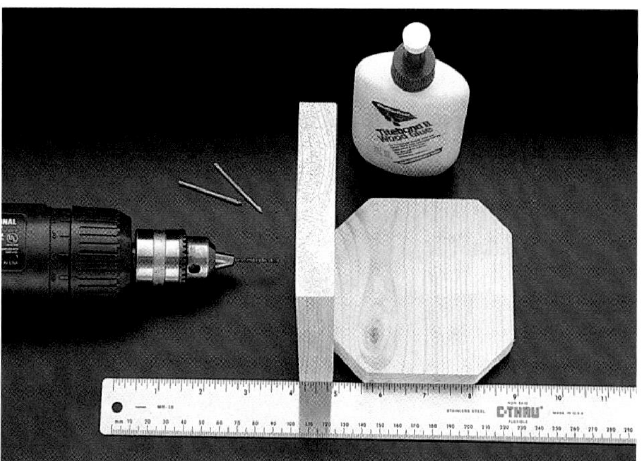

D. *Glue a side piece to the bottom piece. Drill pilot holes and nail the pieces together, using 4d galvanized finish nails.*

E. *Align the remaining side wall, then drive one nail through each side, about ⅝" from the upper edge of the front and back.*

F. *Glue the shorter roof piece to the front and back, aligning the top of the roof with the peak of the house. Position the remaining roof piece, drill pilot holes, and nail the roof in place.*

Step D: Attach the Bottom

1. Apply wood glue to one edge of the bottom piece. Set a side piece in place, so the bottoms of the two pieces are flush. Drill pilot holes and secure the pieces with 4d galvanized finish nails.

2. Apply wood glue to the edges of the side and bottom. Align the front piece and adjust until its edge is flush with the face of the side. Drill pilot holes and secure the front to the side, using 4d finish nails. Repeat this process to attach the back.

Step E: Install the Pivoting Side Wall

Put the remaining side piece in place, but do not glue it. To secure this piece to the front wall and back pieces, drive a nail through the front and another through the back wall, each positioned about ⅝" from the upper edge. This arrangement allows the piece to pivot.

Step F: Add the Roof

1. Apply glue to the upper edges of one side of the front and back. Set the 4¾" × 6½" roof piece on the house with its upper edge aligned with the peak of the house.

2. Apply glue to the 5½" × 6½" roof piece and set it in position. Drill pilot holes and drive nails through the roof and into the front. Repeat to secure the roof to the back of the house.

Step G: Add the Finishing Touches

1. Drill a pilot hole in the edge of the front piece, placed about 1" from the lower edge of the house.

Bird	Diameter of Hole
Carolina Wren	1½"
Chickadee	1⅛"
Downy Woodpecker	1¼"
House Wren & Winter Wren	1" to ½"
Nuthatch	1¼"
Titmouse	1¼"

Screw in a shoulder hook, positioning it to hold the side closed.

2. Sand the birdhouse smooth, and then paint or stain it as desired.

You can embellish this basic birdhouse many ways. There are, however, a few important things to keep in mind: Don't paint or apply preservatives to the inside of the house, the inside edge of the entrance hole, or within 1/4" of the face of the entrance hole. And remember, some birds are wary of bright colors, so stay within medium tones as you choose paint and ornaments. If you live in a warm climate, avoid using black or other very dark colors—they absorb heat and can make the house too hot for birds to inhabit.

3. Attach screw eyes through the roof, near the peak. Attach chains to the screw eyes and hang the birdhouse.

G. *Drill a pilot hole about 1" from the lower edge of the front, and then insert a shoulder hook to secure the pivoting side.*

VARIATION: VERTICALLY-MOUNTED BIRDHOUSE

Cut a piece of 1 × 6 for the back, 5½" × 11¾". Mark a line, 3" from the lower edge, and then drill three pilot holes. Trim diagonally across the lower corners, removing 1" from each.

Nail two narrow wood strips on the back side of this piece. This creates space between the house and the mounting surface, which keeps water from collecting behind the back of the birdhouse.

Continue as in Steps A through G on pages 41 to 42. Align the lower edge of the bottom with the line drawn on the back piece and omit the screw eyes in Step G. To mount the birdhouse, drive screws through the back and into a post, tree, or other structure.

Cut the back piece, drill pilot holes, and trim the lower corners.

Nail two wood strips to the back of the birdhouse. Complete construction as for the hanging birdhouse.

Deck Rail Planter

If the number and variety of containers offered through garden centers and catalogs is any indication, container gardening is more popular now than ever. And no wonder—containers allow you to control soil conditions, move plants as necessary to meet their sun requirements, and brighten otherwise plain areas of your yard or garden. This deck rail planter offers an easy, inexpensive way to turn your deck into an extension of your garden.

The planter, which is designed to hold potted plants, is basically a four-sided bottomless box with spacers that hold the planter in place. The open construction makes it easy to rotate the plants with the seasons. Pots of early pansies can make way for the geraniums, petunias, and marigolds of summer, which in time can yield to chrysanthemums, extending the season long into fall.

Our planter is 10" wide and 42¾" long, but you can build yours to any length you want. If you're building a planter that's more than 32" long, add a center support to keep the boards from warping as they weather.

Before deciding on a specific length for a planter box, determine the size of the pots and saucers you plan to use; then calculate a length that will accommodate an even number of pots with a bit of space in between. Keep in mind that the inside length of a planter without a center support will be 2¼" less than the outside length; in one with a center support, it's 3⅛" less. It might be helpful to draw a diagram (such as the one on page 45), including the pots you plan to use.

When buying lumber, select the straightest, most knot-free boards you can find, and add 10% to the length you need, to allow for trimming. Mark cuts carefully to avoid having knots at cut ends—they're unreliable anchoring points and it's difficult to screw into them.

TOOLS & MATERIALS

- Straightedge
- Tape measure
- Utility knife
- Jig saw or circular saw
- Drill and 3/32" bit
- Cordless screwdriver
- 1 × 8 cedar lumber
- 3" galvanized drywall or deck screws
- 1 5/8" galvanized drywall or deck screws
- Exterior wood glue
- Wood preservatives, stain, or paint

HOW TO BUILD A DECK RAIL PLANTER

Step A: Cut the Front and Back Pieces

Mark a 1 × 8 board at 42¾". To keep the wood from splintering when you cut it, lightly score along the marked line, using a utility knife. Cut this front piece, using a jig saw or circular saw. Use this piece as a template to mark and cut the back.

Step B: Cut the End Pieces & Support Pieces

1. Mark an end piece 8½" long. Score along the marked line and cut the piece. Use this piece as a template to mark the other end piece and the center support (if your planter is more than 32" long).

2. Trim 1" off the bottom of each end piece (and center support, if necessary), so each measures 6¼" × 8½". Set the scraps aside for spacers in Step D.

Step C: Assemble the Main Pieces

1. Mark the placement for three screws, ¾" from one end of the front piece. Place one mark 1" from

A. *Mark the desired lengths and score along the marked lines. Cut the pieces, using a jig saw or circular saw.*

B. *On end pieces and center support, trim 1" from the lower edge, creating 6¼" × 8½" pieces.*

CUTTING LIST

42¾" 1 x 8	(1, for front)
42¾" 1 x 8	(1, for back)
8½" 1 x 8	(2, for ends)
8½" 1 x 8	(1, for support)

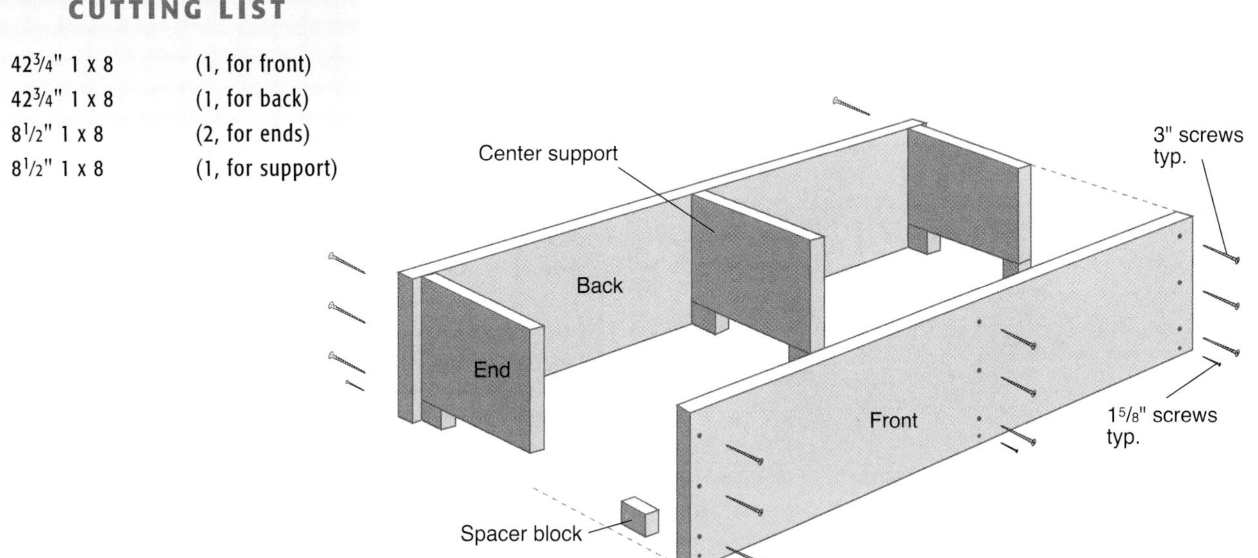

the upper edge, one mark 2" from the lower edge, and one centered between the first two marks. Repeat at the center of the front piece and at the opposite end.

2. Repeat the process for the back piece.

3. Stand one end piece upright and position the front piece against it, extending the front piece 1/4" beyond the end piece. At each mark, drill a pilot hole, using a 3/32" bit. To secure the pieces, drive 3" drywall or deck screws through the front and into the end piece. Repeat the process for the other end piece and the center support.

Step D: Add the Spacers

1. Measure the width of your deck rail and add 1/8" to that measurement. Subtract the total from the inside width of the box. From the scraps set aside in Step B, cut spacers equal to one half this measurement. Cut six spacer blocks—two for each end piece and two for the center support.

2. Glue one spacer block to each side of the end pieces and the center support, offsetting the blocks 1/8" from the front and end pieces. Drill pilot holes and drive a 1 5/8" drywall or deck screw into each.

Step E: Apply a Finish

Apply two coats of primer and then paint the boards. Make sure you let the primer dry thoroughly between coats. Or, if you want the planters to have a more natural appearance, apply wood preservative or exterior wood stain to the inside, outside, and all edges of the boards.

C. *Mark the placement of three screws, and then drill pilot holes at the marked locations. Drive screws through pilot holes, securing both end pieces and the center support.*

PLANTER WIDTH FORMULA

5 1/2" (width of deck rail)	8 1/2" inside width
+1/8"	-5 5/8" of box
----------	----------
5 5/8"	2 7/8"

2 7/8" divided by 2 = 1 7/16" spacer blocks

D. *Attach spacer blocks to each side of the end pieces and the center support, offsetting them 1/8" from the edges of the front and end pieces.*

E. *Apply wood preservative, stain, or paint to all faces and edges of the planter.*

TIP: MAINTAINING A CONTAINER GARDEN

Container gardens are so portable and versatile that they can be located virtually anywhere, even in unexpected areas. An ordinary deck rail can become an herb garden, a stairway can become a flower patch, or a basic privacy fence can come alive with foliage in hanging baskets. You can create an almost instant garden anywhere you can place a planter or hang a basket.

Although container gardens often are filled with well-known annuals, hundreds of plant varieties can be grown in containers. Just remember that the containers must hold enough soil to support the plants, provide adequate drainage, and be placed in locations with appropriate lighting conditions.

Container gardens have a few other requirements. The most important is an increased need for water. It makes sense when you think about it—plants in open ground can extend their roots in search of moisture, but container-grown plants don't have that option. They rely on you to provide consistent moisture.

In warm weather, you may have to water a container garden more than once a day. The general rule is to keep soil moist but not soggy. Damp soil often is darker than dry, and a pot filled with dry soil typically weighs less than one filled with moist soil. Wilting leaves are signs of stress, too, but it's best not to let your plants dry out to the point that they're suffering that much stress.

Water during the early to mid-morning hours to reduce the amount of moisture lost to evaporation and give plants extra strength to withstand the afternoon heat. On hot or windy days, water again at dusk.

In cooler weather, you'll probably only have to water once a week, preferably in the late morning. Avoid watering in the evening if there's any danger of frost.

A CHRISTMAS MEMORY • TRUMAN CAPOTE

Garden Furnishings

Comfortable, attractive furnishings invite visitors into your garden and encourage them to linger. From a bench that provides a comfortable place for two or more people to sit and relax (page 64), to a mosaic table that's alluring on its own or as a place for refreshments (page 56), or recycled treasures (page 54) that provoke fond memories, furnishings add immeasurably to a garden's ambience. With a few simple tools and materials, you can build or reinvent pieces that reflect your interests and abilities and imbue your garden's atmosphere with your personal style.

Furnishings can also provide a source of entertainment, as in the case of the Tabletop Zen Garden (page 68). Zen gardens are intriguing, from the desktop versions in catalogs and gift stores, to the full-scale gardens pictured in magazines. But they're a little like the Three Bears—one's too small and one's just too big to be practical. With these instructions, you can build a version scaled to the proportions of your deck or patio. Guests often sit around mine, sharing quiet conversation and perhaps, a glass of wine, as we rake sand and compose the garden's shells, stones, and other elements.

IN THIS CHAPTER:

Hypertufa Planter

Gardening magazines and catalogs often feature stone or concrete troughs brimming with flowers or planted as alpine gardens. Many of the pieces pictured in magazines are antiques, but others are reproductions that merely look weathered and worn. With all the interest in them, antique versions have become hard to find, and even reproductions are expensive.

With hypertufa, you can create inexpensive, long-lasting planters that resemble aged stone sinks or troughs. Or, if your taste runs more toward contemporary shapes, you can easily create more streamlined pieces. I've experimented with formulas and construction methods (page 102) enough to realize just how versatile hypertufa is and how much fun it is to work with.

You have to plan ahead for this project. It takes several weeks for hypertufa to cure and several more to wash out the alkaline residue enough to use the planter.

TOOLS & MATERIALS

- Tape measure
- Jig saw
- Straightedge
- Drill
- Hacksaw
- Wheelbarrow or mixing trough
- Hammer
- Chisel or paint scraper
- Wire brush
- Propane torch
- 12-quart bucket
- 2"-thick polystyrene insulation board
- $3\frac{1}{2}$" deck screws (40)
- Gaffer's tape
- Scrap of 4"-dia. PVC pipe
- Dust mask
- Gloves
- Portland cement
- Peat moss
- Perlite
- Fiberglass fibers
- Concrete dye (optional)
- Plastic tarp
- Scrap 2 × 4

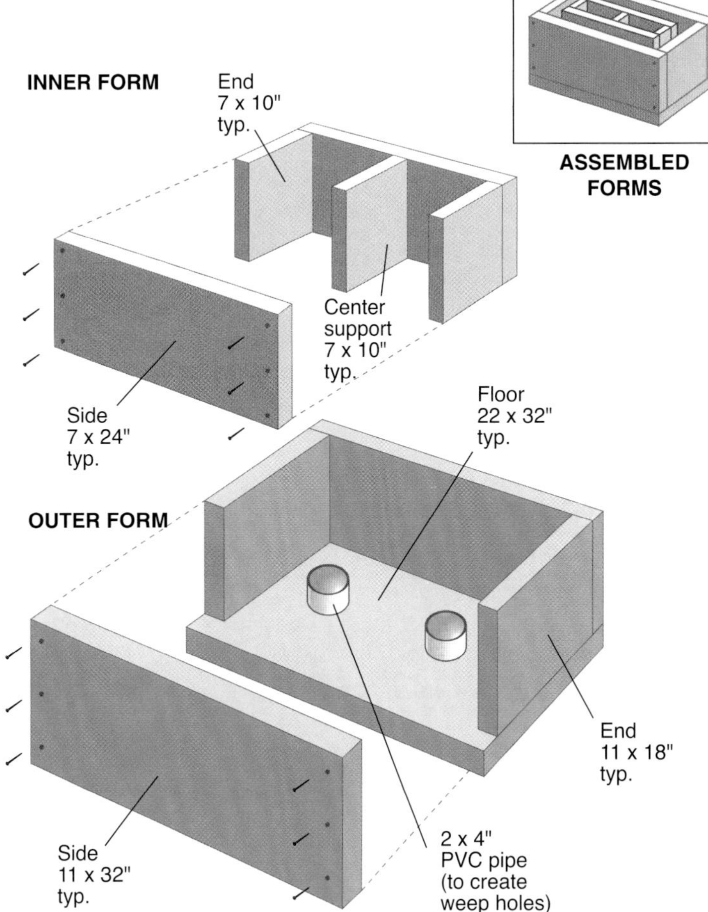

CUTTING LIST

Outer Form	Inner Form
22" × 32" (1, for floor)	7" × 24" (2, for sides)
11" × 32" (2, for sides)	7" × 10" (3, for ends and center support)
11" × 18" (2, for ends)	

HOW TO BUILD A HYPERTUFA PLANTER

Step A: Build the Forms

1. Measure, mark, and cut pieces of 2"-thick polystyrene insulation board to the dimensions in the cutting list above, using a jig saw.

2. To construct the outer form, fit an end piece between the two side pieces and fasten each joint, using three $3\frac{1}{2}$" deck screws. Repeat to fasten the other end. Wrap gaffer's tape entirely around the form. Place one loop of tape near the top and another near the bottom of the form. Set the bottom squarely on top of the resulting rectangle, and then screw and tape it securely in place.

3. Construct the inner form, following the same method .

4. Cut two 2" pieces of 4"-dia. PVC pipe, using a hacksaw, and set them aside.

A. *To construct the forms, fasten the joints with $3\frac{1}{2}$" deck screws; then reinforce them with gaffer's tape.*

Step B: Form the Floor

1. Center the pieces of PVC pipe in the floor of the outer form and press them into the foam; these pipes establish the planter's weep holes.

2. Mix the hypertufa, following the directions on pages 102 to 103. Be sure to wear a dust mask and gloves when handling dry cement mix; also wear gloves when working with wet cement.

3. Pack hypertufa onto the floor of the form, pressing it down firmly and packing it tightly around the pieces of PVC. Continue to add hypertufa until you've created a solid, level, 2"-thick floor.

B. *Pack hypertufa onto the floor of the form; press it down firmly to create a level, 2"-thick floor.*

Step C: Build the Walls

Place the inner form within the outer form, centering it carefully. Add hypertufa between the outer and inner forms, using a scrap 2 × 4 to tamp it down as you go. Try to be consistent in the amount of pressure you use while tamping the hypertufa—the walls of the planter need to be strong enough to withstand the weight and pressure of soil, moisture, and growing plants. Continue adding and tamping the hypertufa until it reaches the top of the forms.

Step D: Allow to Dry & Remove the Forms

1. Cover the planter with a plastic tarp, and let it dry for at least 48 hours. If the weather is exceptionally warm, remove the tarp and mist the planter with water occasionally during the curing process.

2. Remove the tape and screws from the outer form, working carefully so the form can be reused, if desired. If the walls appear to be dry enough to handle without damaging the planter, remove the inner forms. If not, let the planter cure for another 24 hours, then remove the inner form.

You may notice that the planter's surface looks almost hairy, an effect created by the fiberglass in the hypertufa mixture. Don't be concerned about it at this point—the hairy fringe will be removed later.

Step E: Complete the Curing Process

1. Many of the stone planters on the market have a somewhat rustic appearance. If you like that look, this is the time to create it. Working slowly and carefully, use a hammer to round the corners and rough up the edges of the planter.

C. *Center the inner form within the outer form, and then tamp hypertufa between the two, forming the walls.*

D. *After the planter has dried for 48 hours, remove the screws and carefully disassemble the forms.*

2. To add texture, gouge grooves on the sides and ends of the planter, using a chisel or paint scraper. Complete the aging process by brushing the entire planter with a wire brush. Be bold with these aging techniques—the more texture you create, the more time-worn the planter will appear to be.

3. Cover the planter with plastic, and let it cure for about a month. Uncover it at least once a week, and mist it with water to slow down the curing process. Although it's natural to be impatient, don't rush this step. The more slowly the hypertufa cures, the stronger and more durable the planter will be.

4. Unwrap the planter and let it cure outside, uncovered, for several weeks. Periodically wash it down with water to remove some of the alkaline residue of the concrete (which would otherwise endanger the plants grown in the planter). Adding vinegar to the water speeds this process somewhat, but it still takes several weeks. Again, this step is important, so don't rush it.

After the planter has cured outside for several weeks, put it inside, away from any sources of moisture, to cure for several more weeks.

5. When the planter is completely dry, use a propane torch to burn off the hairy fringe on the surface. Move the torch quickly, holding it in each spot no more than a second or two. If pockets of moisture remain, they can get so hot that they explode, leaving pot holes in the planter. To avoid that problem, make sure the planter is dry before you begin, and work quickly with the torch so no significant heat occurs.

E. *Round the edges and corners of the planter with a hammer, and gouge it with a chisel or paint scraper. Brush the entire planter with a wire brush, and then set it outside to cure.*

ENCOURAGING MOSS

Moss helps ornaments blend into a garden as though they've been there forever. If you don't want to wait for moss to form naturally, there are several ways to encourage its growth. These recipes work best if you place the ornaments in moist, shady locations.

• Pour buttermilk over the ornament, and then press patches of fresh moss onto it. Mist the surface occasionally while you wait for new patches of moss to form.

• Generously paint the surface with water from a fish pond or water garden, which generally contains mold spores. Repeat this procedure several times over 24 hours, and then brush on a solution of 2 tablespoons of white school glue dissolved in a quart of water.

• Dissolve 8 ounces of blue clay or porcelain clay in 3 cups of water. Add a cup of fish emulsion fertilizer and a cup of fresh moss. Blend the mixture thoroughly–an old, otherwise unused blender would be ideal–and paint it onto the ornament.

Recycled Treasures

According to Ralph Waldo Emerson, things may be pretty, graceful, rich, elegant, or handsome, but until they speak to the imagination, they're not yet beautiful. I occasionally come across an odd or interesting piece that speaks to my imagination, and sometimes a piece virtually shouts that it would be a beautiful garden ornament.

I found the ironwork pictured below (and on page 55) at a flea market. I was immediately drawn to it, especially because it had stood sentry over the gateway to an Egyptian courtyard for nearly a century. It now provides a backdrop for one of my favorite borders, and to me, it's beautiful.

You can do this in your own garden. Just remember: any piece that speaks to your imagination will work if you find or create the right setting for it.

Before you decide to put a piece to use, assess its condition. Make sure any wood is free of rot and pests. You don't have to rule out clay, ceramic, or masonry pieces that have chips or minor cracks, but avoid pieces with major structural damage. Rust adds character to metal pieces, but edges that are rusted through may be dangerous or unstable.

Not every unique item needs to become a planting container—consider using an unusual piece as sculpture, turning it into a furnishing piece, or adapting it to support other planting containers, such as hanging baskets.

TOOLS & MATERIALS

- Stiff-bristled brush
- Utility knife
- Drill and carbide-tipped bit
- Hand maul
- Horticultural disinfectant
- Horticultural preservative
- Masking tape
- Zinc gauze or fine wire mesh
- Washed pea gravel
- #4 rebar
- Copper wire
- Pressure-treated 2 × 4
- Galvanized deck screws

HOW TO PREPARE PLANTING CONTAINERS

1. Soak the item in clean water for several hours or overnight to loosen any debris. Using a mild detergent and a stiff brush, scrub the entire piece, particularly the surface of the planting area. Rinse thoroughly, and then apply a disinfectant formulated to remove latent fungi or bacterial growth from planting containers. Thoroughly rinse the entire piece again, removing all residue, and then let it dry.

2. Check the piece to see if it needs repair. Look for cracking, chipping, flaking, or other signs of damage that might affect the health of plants in the container. If the piece is wood, prod all surfaces, especially the corners and the bottom, with a utility knife to evaluate it for rot. To protect wood from rot and pests, apply a horticultural preservative.

3. With most pieces, the simplest way to create drainage is to drill three or four holes in the bottom. If the piece is clay or ceramic, you can prevent cracking or chipping by placing a piece of masking tape over the area before you begin drilling, and by using a carbide-tipped bit.

Cover each drainage hole with a section of thin zinc gauze or fine wire mesh. To filter out debris and provide additional drainage, add a layer of washed pea gravel to the container before you add the potting soil and plants.

HOW TO SUPPORT DECORATIVE PIECES

Select a location for the piece; typically, a level site is preferable. Consider the support requirements of the piece and select an appropriate method of securing your treasure so it won't be disturbed by the wind or a playful pet.

- Drive 32" pieces of rebar about 18" into the ground, located at opposite corners of the piece or at other strategic points. Position the piece and use copper wire to secure it to the rebar.
- Cut a pressure-treated 2 × 4 to extend at least 6" beyond each end of the piece to be supported. Drill pilot holes through the bottom of the piece and corresponding ones into the 2 × 4. Align the pilot holes and secure the piece by driving deck screws through the brace and into the piece. Finally, drive spikes through the brace and into the ground, anchoring the piece securely.

Scrub and disinfect items to be used as planting containers. Drill drainage holes, and cover them with thin zinc gauze or fine wire mesh, and then add a 2" layer of washed pea gravel.

Stake or support decorative pieces by wiring them to lengths of rebar driven at least 18" into the ground.

Mosaic Table

Webster's defines composition as "...the arrangement into proper proportion or relation and esp. artistic form." Furnishing outdoor rooms requires an eye for composition, and certain elements are necessary to create the right proportions and form.

One element I use over and over is an end table. Whether placed beside a comfortable chair in a corner of the garden or nestled between a couple of love seats along the edge of a patio, an end table can add the touch that completes an arrangement.

This mosaic table combines two of my favorite activities—recycling unused pieces and playing with color. For the base shown here, we found a table at a garage sale, removed its shabby top and gave the base a quick coat of spray paint. This happens to be a small, square table, but you can adapt the plans to a base of any size or shape. And although we've demonstrated a simple pattern in shades of one color, there's really no limit to the range of colors and designs that will work for this project.

Once you've mastered the basic techniques of doing mosaics, design your own patterns. Anything goes—from simple, inexpensive tile patterns to more elaborate arrangements of seashells, tumbled glass, or decorative stones.

TOOLS & MATERIALS

- Tape measure
- Circular saw or jig saw
- Finishing sander
- Tile nippers
- Rubber mallet
- Masonry file
- Grout float
- Table base
- ½" exterior grade plywood
- Sandpaper
- Wood sealer
- ½" wood screws
- Transfer paper
- Permanent marker
- Safety goggles
- Gloves
- Tile
- Accent stones
- Craft sticks
- Silicone adhesive
- Tile mastic
- Grout
- Grout colorant (optional)
- Grout sponge
- Soft cloth
- Silicone grout sealer
- Paintbrush

A. *Measure the table base and cut a plywood base to match. Seal the plywood and securely attach it to the table base.*

HOW TO BUILD A MOSAIC TABLE

Step A: Prepare the Mosaic Base

1. Measure the table base and determine appropriate dimensions for the mosaic. Mark those dimensions onto exterior-grade plywood, and cut out the base for the mosaic, using a circular saw or jig saw. Lightly sand the plywood.

2. Apply two coats of wood sealer to one side of the plywood base; let it dry thoroughly between coats.

3. Make placement marks on the sealed side of the plywood; use them as guides to position the plywood on the base. Secure the plywood to the table base, using ½" wood screws.

Step B: Enlarge & Transfer the Pattern

1. Using the grid method or a photocopier, enlarge the pattern shown at right.

2. Transfer the pattern to the surface of the plywood base, using transfer paper and a pencil or stylus. To make the pattern easier to see, draw over the traced lines with a permanent marker.

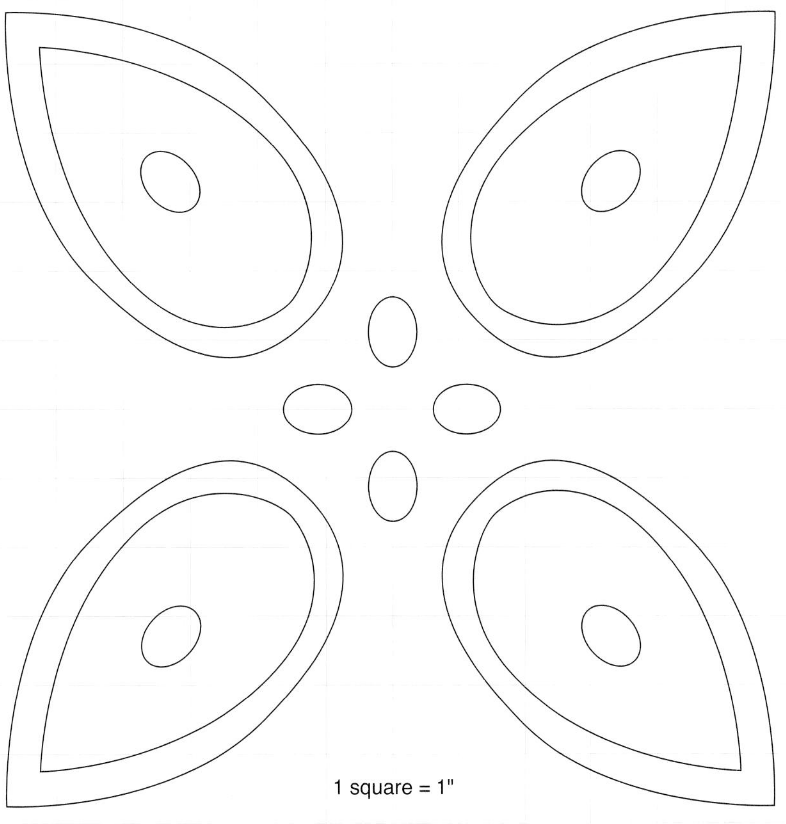

Step C: Apply the Mosaic

1. Place the items to be broken between heavy layers of newsprint or in a heavy paper bag. Wearing safety goggles and heavy gloves, tap the tile with a rubber mallet. It's best to break items of different colors separately to make it easier to select and place colors within the design.

B. *Enlarge the pattern using a grid system or a photocopier; transfer the enlarged pattern to the plywood base.*

2. Cut and shape tiles as necessary, using tile nippers, and use a masonry file to file off any sharp edges. Be sure to wear heavy gloves as you work, at least until you've filed the sharp edges off of the tile.

3. Use silicone adhesive to adhere the media to the plywood base. Wear rubber gloves and spread the adhesive with a craft stick. Glue on the accent stones at the center of the design. Fill in the center of the flower petals with medium-colored pottery shards. Fill the remaining area of the petals with dark-colored pottery shards. Place tile fragments in the background. Arrange the border tiles, alternating the direction of the triangle points. Let the adhesive dry thoroughly, according to manufacturer's directions.

Step D: Set Tile on the Edges

Use silicone adhesive to secure tile along the edges of the table, arranging them to create a uniform edge for the table.

Step E: Grout the Tile

1. Wearing rubber gloves, mix grout and water, according to manufacturer's instructions, usually about three parts grout to one part water. If the spaces between tiles in the mosaic are more than 1/4", be sure to use sanded grout. Grout can't be saved from one project to the next after it's mixed, so unless you're adding grout colorant it's best to mix a little at a time. If you're coloring the grout, mix enough for the entire project at once because it's

C. *After breaking the tile, shape the pieces with tile nippers and file away any sharp edges. Use silicone adhesive to glue the pieces to the plywood base.*

D. *Set tile around the edges of the plywood base; position the tile to create a uniform edge around the table.*

very difficult to match colors from one batch to the next.

2. With a small grout float, spread grout over the mosaic design. Let the grout dry for 5 to 10 minutes.

3. Wipe the excess grout off the surface of the mosaic, using a damp sponge and rinsing it often. Keep rinsing and wiping until the grout is completely gone—if you let grout dry on the surface of the mosaic, it will be very difficult to remove. When you've removed all the grout, let the surface dry.

4. Polish away the haze from any grout residue, using a soft, dry cloth. Let the mosaic dry for 48 hours.

5. To seal the grout and protect it from the elements, apply one or two coats of silicone grout sealer. Follow manufacturer's instructions and let the sealer dry between coats.

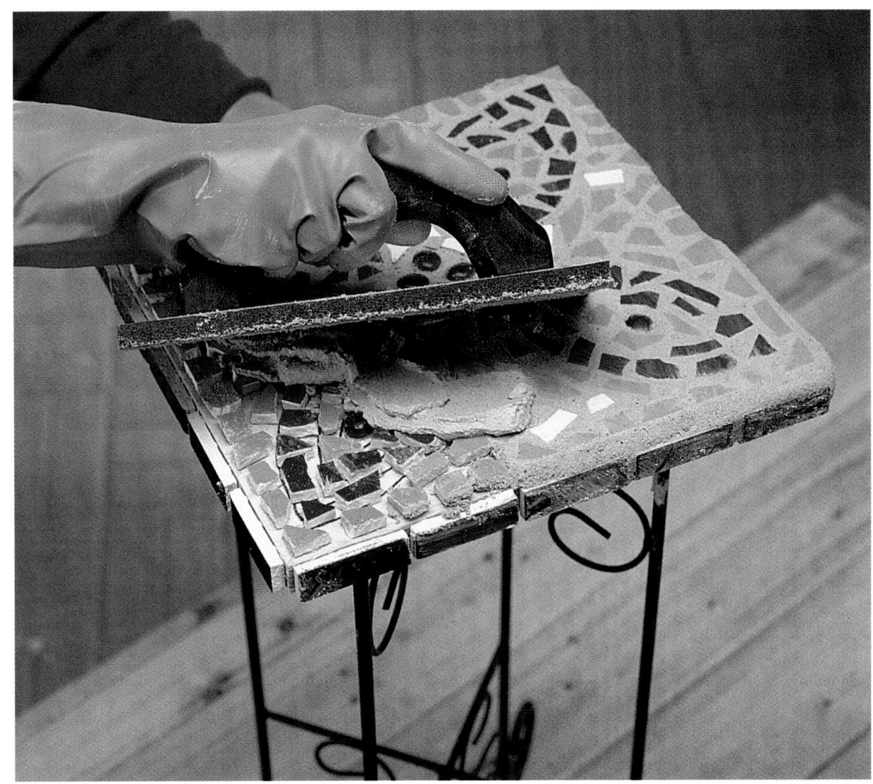

E. *Apply grout, filling cracks completely. Let dry for 5 to 10 minutes, and then rinse away excess grout. Let the mosaic dry for 48 hours; seal it with silicone grout sealer.*

ALTERNATIVE MATERIALS

A wide variety of materials for mosaics, such as the 3/4" square ceramic tiles, faceted stones, and tumbled glass used in this mosaic, are available at craft and hobby stores. To successfully combine materials, establish a color scheme and select a variety of items that complement the scheme.

Many other materials work well for mosaics. To create unique decorative pieces, try using broken china or pottery, buttons, polished pebbles, glass marbles, or seashells.

You can use tile adhesive to secure small tile and other flat items, but you need silicone adhesive for uneven pieces, such as broken pottery or seashells.

Planter Boxes

Decorating a garden is much like decorating a room in your home—it's nice to have pieces that are adaptable enough that you can move them around occasionally and create a completely new look. After all, most of us can't buy new furniture every time we get tired of the way our living rooms look. And we can't build or buy new garden furnishings every time we want to rearrange the garden.

That's one of the reasons this trio of planter boxes works so well. In addition to being handsome — especially when flowers are bursting out of them—they're incredibly adaptable. You can follow these plans to build a terrific trio of planter boxes that will go well with each other and will complement most gardens, patios, and decks. Or you can tailor the plans to suit your needs. For instance, you may want three boxes that are exactly the same size. Or you might want to build several more and use them as a border that encloses a patio or frames a terraced area.

Whatever the dimensions of the boxes, the basic construction steps are the same. If you decide to alter the designs, take a little time to figure out the new dimensions and sketch plans. Then devise a new cutting list and do some planning so you can make efficient use of your wood. To save cutting time, clamp together parts that are the same size and shape, and cut them as a group (called *gang cutting*).

When your planter boxes have worn out their welcome in one spot, you can easily move them to another, perhaps with a fresh coat of stain and new plantings. You can even use the taller boxes to showcase outdoor relief sculptures—a kind of alfresco sculpture gallery.

TOOLS & MATERIALS

- Tape measure
- Circular saw
- Straightedge
- Drill
- Finishing sander
- Miter box and backsaw
- 8 ft. cedar 1 × 2s (3)
- 8 ft. cedar 1 × 4s (6)
- 4 × 8 ft. sheet of ⅝" fir siding
- 2 × 4 ft. piece ¾" CDX plywood
- 1¼" galvanized deck screws
- 1½" galvanized deck screws
- 6d galvanized finish nails
- Exterior wood stain
- Paintbrush

DIMENSIONS

Front Bin Overall Size
12" High
18" Wide
24" Long

Back Bin Overall Size
24" High
18" Wide
12" Long

Middle Bin Overall Size
18" High
18" Wide
12" Long

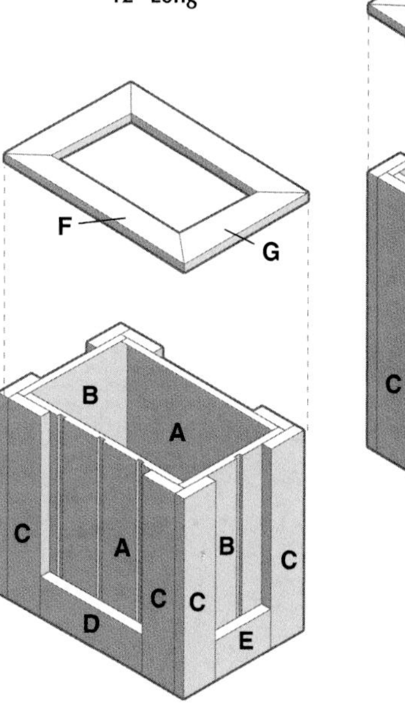

FRONT BIN

MIDDLE BIN

BACK BIN

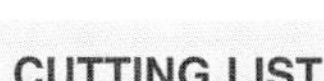
CUTTING LIST

Key	Part	Front Bin Dimension	Pcs.	Middle Bin Dimension	Pcs.	Back Bin Dimension	Pcs.	Material
A	End panel	⅝ × 15 × 11⅛"	2	⅝ × 15 × 17⅛"	2	⅝ × 15 × 23⅛"	2	Siding
B	Side panel	⅝ × 22¼ × 11⅛"	2	⅝ × 10¼ × 17⅛"	2	⅝ × 10¼ × 23⅛"	2	Siding
C	Corner trim	⅞ × 3½ × 11⅛"	8	⅞ × 3½ × 17⅛"	8	⅞ × 3½ × 23⅛"	8	Cedar
D	Bottom trim	⅞ × 3½ × 9¼"	2	⅞ × 3½ × 9¼"	2	⅞ × 3½ × 9¼"	2	Cedar
E	Bottom trim	⅞ × 3½ × 17"	2	⅞ × 3½ × 5"	2	⅞ × 3½ × 5"	2	Cedar
F	Top cap	⅞ × 1½ × 18"	2	⅞ × 1½ × 18"	2	⅞ × 1½ × 18"	2	Cedar
G	Top cap	⅞ × 1½ × 24"	2	⅞ × 1½ × 12"	2	⅞ × 1½ × 12"	2	Cedar
H	Bottom panel	¾ × 14½ × 19½"	1	¾ × 14½ × 8½"	1	¾ × 14½ × 8½"	1	Plywood
I	Cleat	⅞ × 1½ × 12"	2	⅞ × 1½ × 12"	2	⅞ × 1½ × 12"	2	Cedar

Note: Measurements reflect the actual size of dimension lumber.

HOW TO BUILD PLANTER BOXES

Step A: Make & Assemble the Box Panels

1. Following the cutting list on page 61, cut the end panels (A) and side panels (B), using a circular saw and a straightedge cutting guide.

2. Put one end panel face-down on your work surface, butting it up against the side panel, face-side-out. Mark positions and drill several counterbored 3/32" pilot holes in the side panel.

3. Fasten the side panel to the end panel with 1½" deck screws. Repeat this process to fasten a second side panel to the end panel.

4. Put the remaining end panel face-down on the work surface. Take the assembled pieces and place the open end over the second end panel, side panels flush with the end-panel edges. Drill counterbored pilot holes in the side panels, and attach the side panels to the end panel, using deck screws.

Step B: Attach the Trim

1. Cut the corner trim (C) to length. Overlap the edges of the corner trim pieces at the corner, forming a square butt joint. Fasten the corner trim pieces to the panels by driving 1¼" deck screws through the inside faces of the panels and into the corner pieces.

2. To provide extra support, drive screws or galvanized finish nails through the overlapping corner trim pieces and into the edges of the adjacent trim piece.

3. Cut the bottom trim pieces (D, E) to length. Fasten them to the end and side panels, between the corner trim pieces. Drive 1¼" deck screws through the side and end panels and into the bottom trim pieces.

4. Cut the top caps (F, G) to length. Cut 45° miters at both ends of one cap piece, using a miter box and back saw.

5. Tack the mitered cap piece to the top edge of the planter, with the outside edges flush with the outer edges of the corner trim pieces. For a proper fit, use this cap piece to guide the marking and cutting of the miters on the other cap pieces.

6. Miter both ends of each piece. Tack it to the box so it makes a square corner with the previously installed piece. If the corners don't fit just right, loosen the pieces, and adjust them until everything is square.

7. Permanently attach all the cap pieces to the box, using 6d galvanized finish nails.

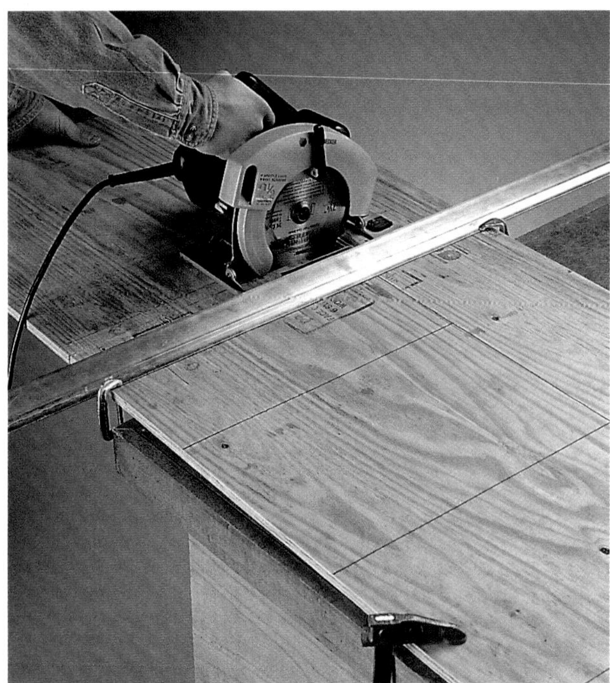

A. *Cut the end panels and side panels to size.*

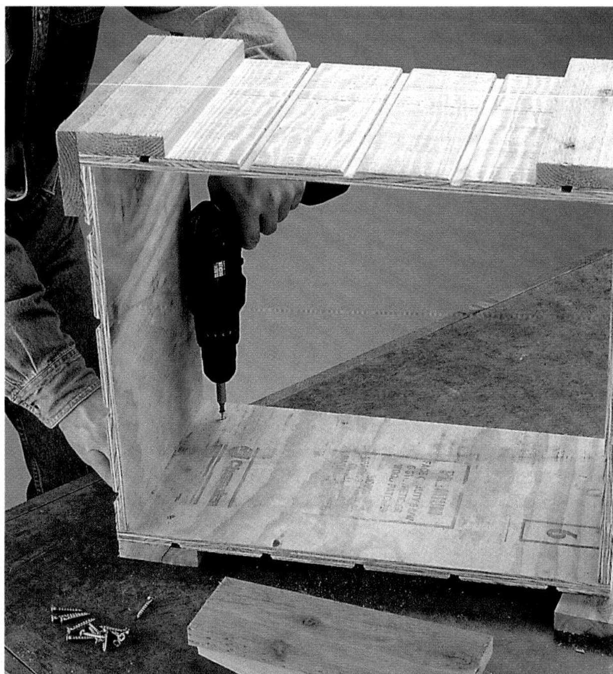

B. *Drive screws through the inside faces of the panels to fasten the corner trim pieces.*

Step C: Install the Box Bottom & Finish the Planter

1. Cut the cleats (I) to length, and screw them to the end panels with 1½" deck screws. On taller planters, it's best to mount the cleats higher on the panels so you won't need as much soil to fill the box—a savings in cost and weight. In that case, add cleats on the side panels for extra support.
2. Cut the bottom panel (H) to size from ¾"-thick CDX plywood. Drill several 1"-diameter weep holes in this panel. Set the panel onto the cleats—it does not need to be fastened in place.
3. Using a finishing sander, remove rough spots and splinters from all edges and surfaces. Apply two or three coats of exterior wood stain to all surfaces, and let the planter dry.

C. *Cut the cleats to length and screw them into the end panels.*

TIPS: SIMPLIFY PLANTING & MAINTENANCE

To help keep planter boxes from becoming discolored, line them with landscape fabric before adding soil. Simply cut a piece of fabric large enough to wrap the box as if you were gift-wrapping it, and then fold it to fit inside the box. Staple the fabric at the top of the box and trim off the excess. Add a 2" layer of gravel, and then add potting soil and plants.

If your yard or garden is partially shaded, you may want to add wheels or casters to your planter boxes so you can move them to follow the sun; casters also make it easier to bring the planters indoors during cold weather. Be sure to use locking wheels or casters with brass or plastic housings.

If you're not experienced at arranging color combinations, start with a simple approach. Stay within the basic hot (red, yellow, and orange) or cool (blue, purple, and green) color families to create visual harmony. You can plant a collection of flowers and foliage in your favorite color or try combining a variety of hues of the same color. If you want to add contrast, add some plants in neutral tones.

Proportion, or the size and scale of plants in relationship to one another and the container, is another important component of successful plantings. In general, plant tall plants in large containers and low-lying plants in smaller ones. To achieve balance, use a dominant plant to establish a focal point, and then fill in around it with a combination of colors, textures, and shapes.

Before purchasing plants for any container, consider their preferred growing conditions. Grouping plants with similar soil, watering, and fertilization requirements simplifies your work during the growing season.

Garden Bench

In much the same way paths suggest that we wander, benches invite us to linger, to contemplate, to savor. For those of us who usually view our gardens from our knees, or who mainly see them as works in progress, benches offer a different perspective, a change of view and attitude. In my garden, benches remind me to relax and enjoy the beauty I am helping to create.

In *The Principles of Gardening*, Hugh Johnson says that garden benches should always look permanent; deliberately placed. One way to achieve that look is to start with a simple design such as this cedar bench. It has the sort of solid simplicity that suggests permanence. And the color of the cedar blends effortlessly into surrounding trees, flowers, and foliage, adding to the impression that the bench is and always will be an essential part of the garden.

Placing a bench deliberately is important, but not complicated. Walk around the garden and think about where you stop to rest, to enjoy a special view, or to appreciate pleasant fragrances. Take note of where visitors pause, and consider what draws them to those spots. A bench can provide a place for the eyes to rest, as well as the body. As you wander, imagine how you might use a bench to draw the eye down a path or into a quiet corner.

With its subtle design, this easy-to-build bench lends itself to being used in combination with other ornaments or furnishings. Flank the ends with cedar planter boxes (page 62) or a copper trellis (page 82) to create a lovely focal point at the edge of a bed or border.

TOOLS & MATERIALS

- Circular saw
- Drill
- Tape measure
- Hammer
- Long metal ruler
- Jig saw
- Finishing sander
- 1½" deck screws
- 2½" deck screws
- Exterior wood glue
- Casing nails (3)
- Wood sealer/stain
- 1 × 4 × 12' cedar (1)
- 2 × 2 × 6' cedar (1)
- 2 × 2 × 10' cedar (4)
- 2 × 4 × 6' cedar (1)
- 2 × 6 × 10' cedar (1)
- 2 × 8 × 6' cedar (1)

HOW TO BUILD A GARDEN BENCH

Step A: Begin the Leg Assemblies & Attach the Trestle

1. Cut the leg halves (A), cleats (B), and trestle (D) to length. Sandwich one leg half between two cleats so the cleats are flush with the top and the outside edge of the leg half. Then join the parts by driving four 1½" deck screws through each cleat and into the leg half. Assemble two more cleats with a leg half in the same fashion.

2. Stand the two assemblies on their sides, with the open ends of the cleat pointing upward. Arrange the assemblies so they are roughly 4 ft. apart. Set the trestle onto the inner edges of the leg halves, pressed flush against the bottoms of the cleats.

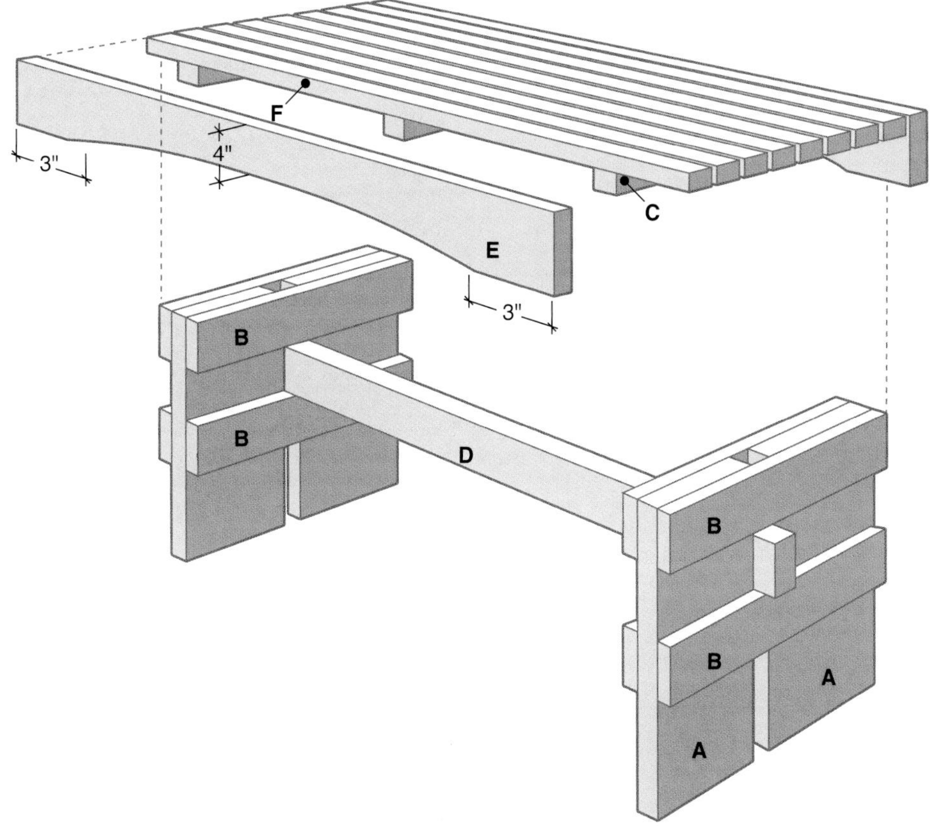

CUTTING LIST

Key	Part	Dimension	Pcs.	Material	Key	Part	Dimension	Pcs.	Material
A	Leg half	1½ × 7¼ × 14½"	4	Cedar	D	Trestle	1½ × 3½ × 60"	1	Cedar
B	Cleat	¾ × 3½ × 16"	8	Cedar	E	Apron	1½ × 5½ × 60"	2	Cedar
C	Brace	1½ × 1½ × 16"	3	Cedar	F	Slat	1½ × 1½ × 60"	8	Cedar

Note: Measurements reflect the actual size of dimension lumber.

A. *Position the trestle against the leg half and the cleats, overhanging the leg half by 1½". Attach the trestle with glue and 2½" screws.*

B. *Attach the remaining leg half to the cleats on both ends to complete the leg assembly.*

C. *Attach the outer brace for the seat slats directly to the inside faces of the cleats.*

Adjust the position of the assemblies so the trestle overhangs the leg half by 1½" at each end. Fasten the trestle to each leg half with glue and 2½" deck screws.

3. Attach another pair of cleats to each leg half directly below the first pair, positioned so each cleat is snug against the bottom of the trestle.

Step B: Complete the Leg Assemblies

Slide the other leg half between the cleats, keeping the top edge flush with the upper cleats. Join the leg halves with the cleats, using glue and 2½" deck screws.

Step C: Add the Braces

Cut the braces (C) to length. Fasten one brace to the inner top cleat on each leg assembly so the tops are flush.

Step D: Shape the Aprons

1. Cut the aprons (E) to length.

2. Lay out the arch onto one apron, starting 3" from each end. The peak of the arch, located over the midpoint of the apron, should be 1½" up from the bottom edge.

3. Draw a smooth, even arch by driving one casing nail at the peak of the arch and one at each of the starting points. Slip a long metal ruler behind the nails at the starting points and in front of the nail at the peak to create a smooth arch. Then trace along the inside of the ruler to mark a cutting line.

4. Cut along the line with a jig saw; then sand the cut smooth.

5. Trace the profile of the arch onto the other apron; make and sand the cut.

TIP: LEVELING LEGS

Sometimes our best efforts produce furniture that wobbles because it's not quite level. Here's a trick for leveling furniture:

Set a plastic wading pool on a flat plywood surface. Add shims under the plywood surface until the floor of the wading pool is exactly level.

Fill the pool with about ¼" of water. Set the piece of furniture in the pool, and then remove it quickly. Mark the top of the waterline on each leg. Use these marks as cutting lines to trim the legs to exactly level.

D. *Pin a long, flexible ruler between casing nails, and then trace a smooth arch onto the aprons.*

E. *Attach a 2 × 2 slat to the top, inside edge of each apron, using glue and 2½" deck screws.*

Step E: Add Slats to the Aprons

Cut the slats (F) to length. Attach a slat to the top, inside edge of each apron, using glue and deck screws.

Step F: Install the Aprons & Slats

1. Apply glue at each end, on the bottom sides, of the attached slats. Flip the leg and trestle assembly, and position it flush with the aprons so that it rests on the glue on the bottoms of the two slats. The aprons should extend 1½" beyond the legs at each end of the bench. Drive 2½" deck screws through the braces and into both slats.

2. Position the middle brace between aprons, centered end to end. Attach it to the two side slats with glue and deck screws.

3. Position the six remaining slats on the braces, using ½"-thick spacers to help you create equal gaps between them. Attach the slats with glue and drive 2½" deck screws up through the braces and into each slat.

4. Sand the slats smooth with progressively finer sandpaper. Wipe away the sanding residue with a rag dipped in mineral spirits. Let the bench dry. Apply a finish of your choice—a clear wood sealer to protect the cedar without altering the color, or stain to provide deeper color for the cedar.

F. *Attach the seat slats with glue and 2½" deck screws. Insert ½"-thick spacers to help set gaps between the slats.*

TIP: COUNTERSINKING SCREWS

Take extra care to completely countersink screw heads whenever you are building furnishings that will be used as seating. When sinking galvanized deck screws, use a combination countersink/piloting bit that drills a 3⁄32"-dia. pilot hole.

Tabletop Zen Garden

Every culture has a different idea of what a garden ought to be—as characteristic as its national cuisine. One that I treasure is the classic Japanese garden. In common with art and architecture in Japan, its finest gardens are breathtakingly subtle and understated. They speak to you with a quiet spirituality. I like to think of them as haiku poems formed out of rocks, sand, wood, and plant material—simple, but profound.

For most of us, building a full-scale Japanese garden isn't practical—our gardens often double as outdoor living spaces in ways that aren't suited to the structure of a Zen garden. But this tabletop version contains the same basic elements and offers opportunities for peaceful contemplation and reflection without requiring a huge investment of time or money. Besides that, it's just plain fun—you can design patterns, rake sand, and rearrange elements to your heart's content.

It's best to use redwood or cedar lumber for the table. You can seal the lumber to maintain its fresh color or let it weather to a rustic gray—either is well suited to the earth-tone color schemes typical of Zen gardens.

Visualize your tabletop garden as a larger landscape and set the stage with sand or fine gravel. Then fill it with rocks, driftwood, an oriental sculpture, and maybe a bonsai tree or a tiny palm. But take care not to overfill it—you need room to "draw" gently curving patterns in the sand.

TOOLS & MATERIALS

- Tape measure
- Circular saw
- Drill
- Finishing sander
- Staple gun
- Utility knife
- 8 ft. cedar or redwood 2 × 4s (5)
- 8 ft. cedar or redwood 1 × 4s (2)
- ¾" CDX plywood, at least 34" × 44"
- Exterior wood glue
- ¼ × 3½" carriage bolts (8)
- 1½" galvanized deck screws
- 2" galvanized deck screws
- 2½" galvanized deck screws
- Exterior wood sealer
- Landscape fabric
- Nylon window screen
- Fine sand or gravel
- Decorative objects

HOW TO BUILD A TABLETOP ZEN GARDEN

Step A: Assemble End Units

1. Cut legs (A), top supports (C), and braces (D) to length, following the cutting list below.
2. Attach a top support to the top, inner sides of each pair of legs, using exterior wood glue and 2½" deck screws. Let the glue dry.
3. Attach a brace across each leg pair, placing the bottom of the brace 6" from the bottom of the legs. Make sure the end unit is square, and secure the brace with glue and 2½" deck screws. Let the glue dry.

Step B: Join End Units to Form Table Base

1. Cut rails (B) and stretcher (E), following the cutting list (below, left).

***A.** Attach a brace to each pair of legs, placing the bottom of the brace 6" from the bottom of the leg.*

½" weep holes typ.
1½" deck screw typ.
F
G
H
G
F
2" deck screw typ.
1½" deck screw typ.
C
B
C
C
D
E
¼ x 3½" carriage bolt typ.
B
2" deck screw typ.
D
A
2½" deck screw typ.

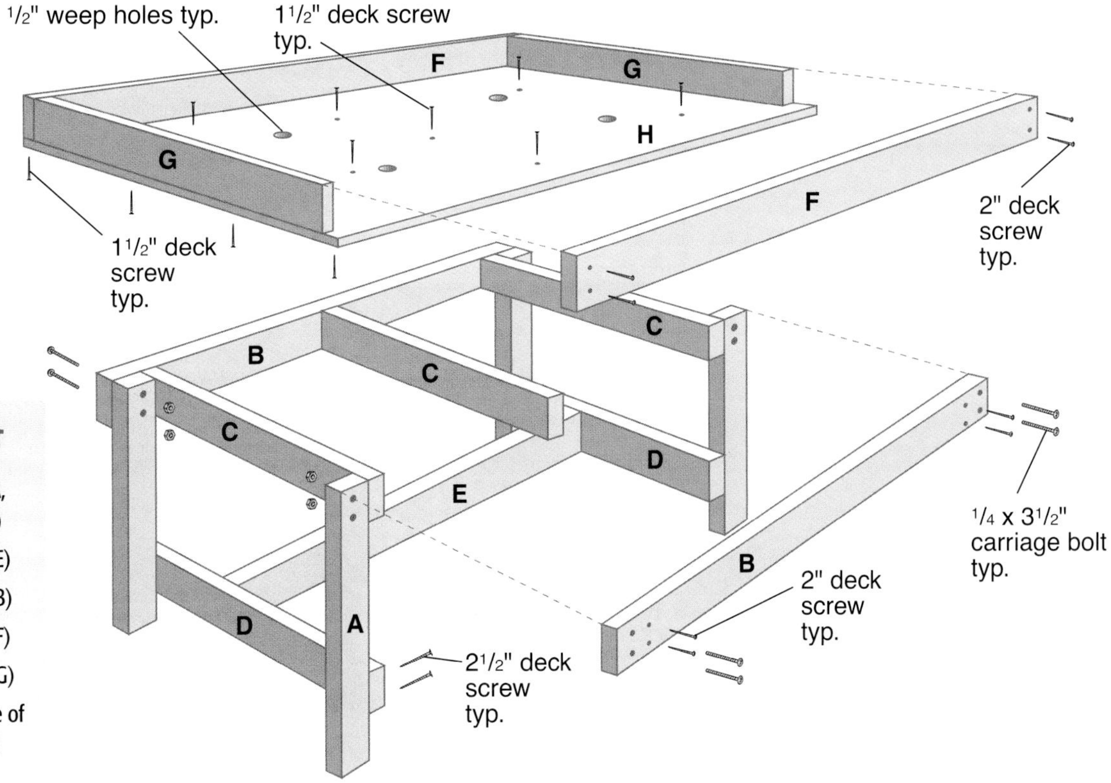

CUTTING LIST

A, C, D	29" 2 × 4 (4 for A, 3 for C, & 2 for D)
E	32" 2 × 4 (1, for E)
B	42" 2 × 4 (2, for B)
F	44" 1 × 4 (2, for F)
G	32" 1 × 4 (2, for G)
H	33½" × 44" piece of ¾" CDX plywood (1, for H)

2. Apply glue to the outside top areas of the end units, where the rails will connect. Attach the rails to the top supports with 2½" deck screws. Let the glue dry.

3. Drill ¼" holes into the ends of the rails and through the tops of the legs. Put a ¼" × 3½" carriage bolt through each hole from the outside and fasten each with a washer and nut.

4. Apply glue to both ends of the stretcher, and center it between the two braces. Secure the stretcher to the braces, using 2½" deck screws.

5. Attach the third top support midway between the rails with glue and 2½" deck screws. The top of the support should be flush with the tops of the rails and other supports. This provides extra strength to support the weight of the sand.

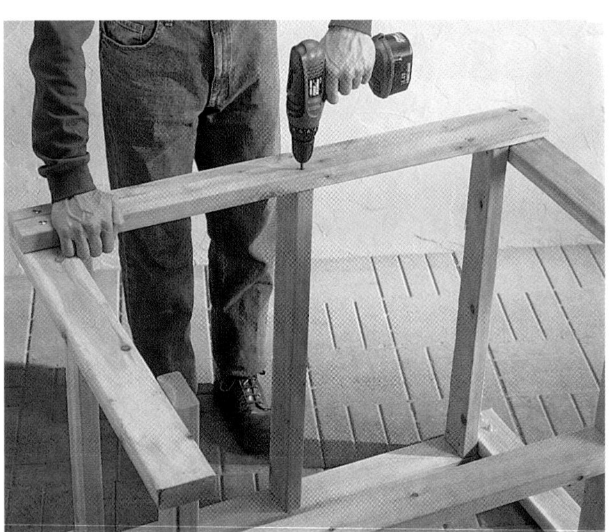

B. *Turn the base on its side, and attach rails to the top supports, using glue and 2" deck screws.*

Step C: Assemble the Tray Tabletop

1. Cut the frame sides (F) and frame ends (G) to size. Attach the frame ends to the frame sides with glue and 2" deck screws driven through the frame sides and into the frame ends.

2. Cut ¾" CDX plywood to size for the tray bottom (H). Apply two coats of exterior wood sealer, and let it dry.

3. With the finished frame resting on a flat surface, position the tray bottom over the frame with all outside edges flush. Drive 1½" deck screws through the tray bottom and into frame.

Step D: Attach the Tray to the Base

1. Center the tray on top of the base. Measure carefully, and mark where the tray bottom rests directly on top of the rails and three top supports.

2. Drive 1½" deck screws through the tray bottom and into the rails and top supports in at least two locations for each rail and support.

Step E: Finish the Tabletop

1. Drill ½" weep holes through the tray bottom in four spots. Cut small pieces of nylon screen, and glue or staple one piece over each drainage hole.

2. Using a finishing sander or sandpaper block, smooth all rough surfaces. If desired, apply an exterior wood sealer to all surfaces, and let it

C. *Set the tray bottom onto the table frame, and secure it, using 1½" deck screws.*

D. *Turn the tray over, and drive 1½" deck screws through the tray bottom and into the rails and top supports.*

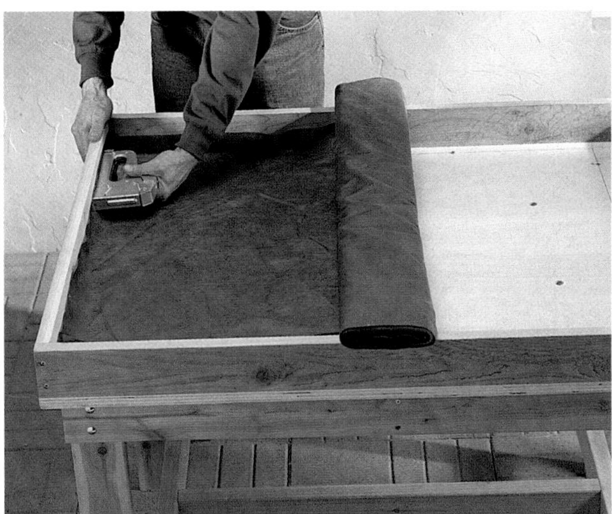

E. *Staple down the edges of the landscape fabric, extending it no more than 2½" above the tray bottom.*

F. *Arrange stones, driftwood, and other decorative objects in the garden. Rake the sand into a pleasing pattern.*

dry thoroughly.

3. Cut a piece of landscape fabric several inches larger in dimension than the tray tabletop. Tuck the fabric into the tray tabletop and tack down the corners with a staple gun. Then staple the edges no higher than 2½" above the tray bottom. Trim the landscape fabric just above the staples, using a utility knife.

Step F: Arrange the Elements

Put the table in place and fill the tabletop with clean, dry sand or gravel—covering the fabric. Experiment with placing stones, pieces of driftwood, or other decorative objects. Use a miniature rake or other appropriate tool to make curved patterns in the sand.

VARIATION: WATERSCAPE

Japanese gardens convey the idea of larger landscapes in confined spaces, often by using dwarf trees and shrubs. They sometimes create the illusion of a gentle waterscape by using raked patterns around "islands" of mounded sand, stones, or gravel. Or they may use an actual watercourse and miniature lake set amidst "mountains" and "forests." They frequently contain small buildings that can be used as places for rest and contemplation.

A fine Japanese garden is more the work of an artist than a gardener. Designing a good one requires both careful thought and spontaneity–very much a case of less being more.

Japanese gardens are miracles of subtlety and grace–full-sized landscapes translated into small, breathtaking spaces.

Trellises & Arbors

As with people, the most interesting gardens are multi-dimensional. Uninterrupted expanses, even beautiful ones, just don't have the allure of spaces punctuated with vertical elements.

Trellises, arbors, and gates add interest to a garden no matter what the season. In springtime they provide backdrops for bright bursts of low-growing color; in summer they showcase the lush growth of vines and climbers; in autumn they frame dramatic views; and in winter they lend shape to the sleeping landscape, particularly in climates where snow transforms their basic forms into fanciful sculpture.

Different styles of trellises and arbors lend themselves to different types of climbing plants. For example, a rustic arbor (page 88) looks wonderful when supporting the luxuriant growth of an annual vine such as a morning glory, or crowned with a potato vine. On the other hand, the lattice pattern of a post and wire trellis would be overwhelmed by such abundance—it's better suited to the more refined growth of a twining vine such as a winter creeper. The weathered patina of a copper trellis (page 82) is spectacular when offset by a riotous pink climbing rose such as Bubble Bath; brick pillars (page 92) work with almost any climber or rambler.

Many of these projects are similar to trellises and arbors that cost hundreds of dollars in catalogs or retail stores. The cost of materials for them, however, ranges from virtually nothing for the rustic arbor to under $75 for the largest copper trellis. Each uses simple construction techniques and inexpensive, readily-available materials. What could be better?

IN THIS CHAPTER:

Lath Trellis

When you want to showcase a climbing plant with spectacular blossoms or foliage, the trellis shouldn't fight for attention. In those situations, these simple lath trellises are perfect.

They're also easy to build, using parting stop for the vertical legs and wide lath (sometimes called lattice) for the horizontal supports. Just secure a horizontal lath piece to both the front and back of the trellis for all but the bottom horizontal support. Then trim the trellis with motifs, such as squares, diamonds, and arrows, cut from screen molding. Parting stop, lath, and screen molding are readily available at home centers.

Although this project gives directions for a specific trellis, the basic plan can be adapted in many ways. When designing a trellis, be sure to take into consideration the space where it will be displayed and the anticipated height of the climbing plants. To make your design more interesting, stagger the lengths of the vertical legs. An odd number of legs is usually more attractive than an even number. It's important to support tall trellises with three horizontal pieces of lath.

Experiment with ideas and sketch possible designs until you find a pleasing arrangement. You can even customize trellis motifs to repeat a theme or design found in surrounding elements, such as furniture or fences.

For a subtle look, you can paint a trellis to match the background surface. Or, to make a design statement year-round, paint the trellis in a color that contrasts with the background.

TOOLS & MATERIALS

- Drill
- Miter saw
- Aviation snips
- 1/2" × 3/4" pine parting stop
- 1/4" × 1 3/8" pine lath
- 1/4" × 3/4" pine or oak screen moldings
- Exterior wood glue
- #19 × 1/2" wire brads
- Exterior primer
- Exterior paint
- Wire clothes hanger or #3 rebar (2 pieces)

HOW TO BUILD A LATH TRELLIS

Step A: Create a Plan

Sketch the trellis to scale. Allow 4" to 8" between each pair of vertical legs. The finished width of the trellis will equal the sum of the distance between the vertical legs plus 3/4" for each vertical leg. Plan to position one horizontal support at the bottom, one about two-thirds of the way up, and another about 2" from the top. Include additional supports if necessary.

Step B: Cut & Arrange the Pieces

1. Draw a full-size pattern of the basic trellis. Cut 3/4" strips of paper and experiment with screen molding motifs. To help keep the brads from splitting the wood when you secure the screen molding, make sure the ends of the design motifs extend beyond the legs of the trellis .

2. Make paper patterns for the motifs, marking the lines for miter cuts on both the upper and lower pattern pieces.

3. Mark and cut the parting stop to the desired length for each vertical leg. For the horizontal supports on the back of the trellis, cut pieces of lath equal to the finished width of the trellis. (You'll cut the remaining horizontal supports for the front of the trellis later.)

4. Working on a smooth, flat surface, arrange the vertical legs with the bottom of all the legs aligned. Place the horizontal supports over the legs, as determined by your design.

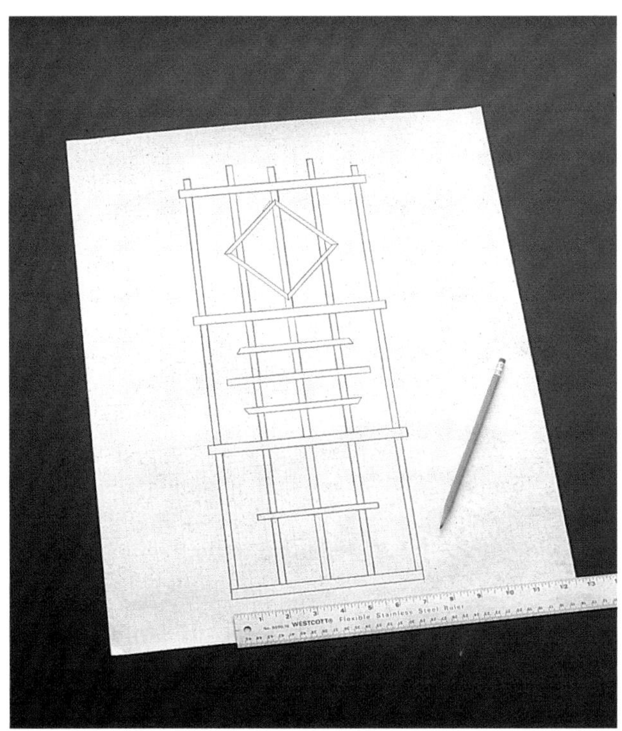

A. *Sketch the trellis to scale.*

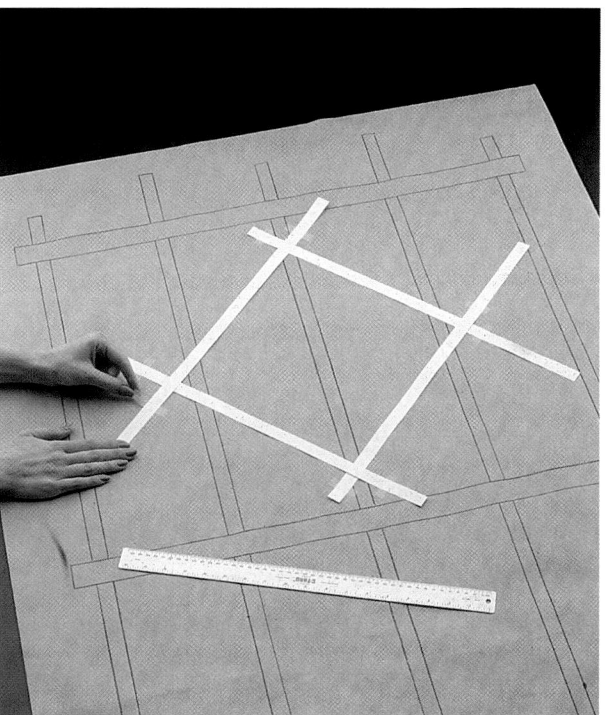

B. *Create a full-size pattern of the trellis. Take measurements and create pattern pieces.*

C. *Position lath over the horizontal supports, extending 1" beyond the legs on each side. Glue and nail these pieces in place.*

D. *Apply exterior primer to both sides of the trellis, then paint it as desired. When the trellis is dry, mount it securely.*

Step C: Construct the Trellis

1. Glue and nail the bottom horizontal support to the legs, securing it with two brads at each joint. Start at one side and work toward the opposite side, staggering the placement of the nails to keep the wood from splitting. Secure the remaining horizontal supports in the same fashion.

2. Cut pieces of lath 2" longer than the width of the trellis. Turn the trellis over and position this lath over the top and middle horizontal supports, extending 1" beyond the legs on each side. Secure each piece of lath with exterior wood glue and a brad driven at each vertical leg.

3. Transfer the markings from the motif patterns (created in Step A) to the screen moldings and cut the pieces necessary for your design. To save time and ensure uniform lengths, clamp together sets of molding strips and cut them in tandem.

4. Glue the screen molding to the trellis. When the glue is tacky, drive brads wherever the screen molding overlaps a leg; place a scrap of lath under the trellis to support it while you drive the brads.

Step D: Finish & Mount the Trellis

1. Apply exterior primer to both sides of the trellis and let it dry. Paint as desired.

2. Mount the trellis, using one of the following methods.

Surface mount: Cut a clothes hanger, using aviation snips; form two loops. Position the trellis against a wall or fence. Use the wire loops to stake the bottom of the trellis, placing one wire loop over each end of the bottom horizontal support. Drill pilot holes in the wall or fence, one hole at each side of the trellis, near the top. Install shoulder hooks to secure the trellis in position.

Freestanding mount: Drive two pieces of #3 rebar into the ground, one at each edge of the trellis. Secure the trellis to the stakes at several points on each side, using plastic-coated wire. The stakes should be buried at least 12" inches beneath the soil and extend above ground to at least half the height of the trellis.

CLIMBING PLANTS

ANNUALS	PERENNIALS
Asarina (Climbing Snapdragon)	Clematis
Morning Glory	Climbing Hydrangea
Nasturtium	Climbing Rose
Scarlet Runner Bean	Dutchman's Pipe
Sweet Pea	Porcelainberry
	Silver Lace Vine

VARIATIONS: WINDOW TRELLIS

To surround a window with foliage without completely obscuring the view, you can build a window trellis (as shown at right). First, measure the window, decide on the dimensions of the trellis and draw a sketch. Make the trellis at least 2" wider than the window and plan to place the upper edge of the top horizontal support just below the bottom of the window. Extend the outer legs of the trellis to support the string portion of the trellis.

Cut the pieces and assemble the trellis as in Step B (page 75). Mark the outer legs at the upper edge of the top horizontal support.

Mark holes on the inside face of the outer legs, indicating 3" to 4" intervals from the horizontal support to the top of the trellis. Drill a hole at each of these marks, using a 1/16" drill bit.

Put the outer legs in position and assemble the trellis as in Steps B and C (page 75). Mount the trellis (Step D, page 76).

Lace monofilament fishing line through the drilled holes, starting at the top of the legs and carrying the line from side to side of the trellis in the same way you would lace a shoe. Cut the line, leaving excess at the ends. Wrap the fishing line around the outer leg of the trellis and tie it in a knot; pull the line taut and tie off the remaining end.

Combine lath and string or nylon fishing line to create a trellis. Train vines to surround the window with foliage.

Discarded wrought iron pieces, such as this window guard (above), old gates, or pieces of fence, are almost instant trellises. Simply mount the piece to some support (page 55) and add plants.

You can make a rustic trellis (left), using both straight and curved branches. Secure the branches with nails or wrap joints with wire. If you plan to shape areas of the trellis, select green branches and construct the trellis as soon as possible after cutting the branches–green, freshly-cut branches are much easier to bend and shape than older, drier branches.

Post & Wire Trellis

The gardens I most admire often seem to be studies in contrast. Great gardeners blend and contrast plant forms, colors, and textures, using each to its greatest advantage. Texture is an important element of this design equation and the reason I originally devised a post and wire trellis.

To create the illusion of depth in a shallow planting bed at the back of my yard, I wanted to use a vertical display of fine-textured foliage as a backdrop for several plants with large, coarse leaves. Although many trellises are designed to support a riot of flowers or a rambunctious layer of foliage, few provide an adequate showcase for the type of delicate texture I had in mind.

It was a challenge to design a trellis that accomplished this mission, matched my construction abilities, and fell within my budget. The solution turned out to be remarkably simple. I topped cedar posts with decorative finials and strung a lattice of plastic-coated wire between them, creating a trellis that would be ideal for many garden settings. The construction is simple, the materials are inexpensive, and the finished effect is stunning.

The best plants for this trellis are twining climbers with small leaves. Among annual vines you can try sweet pea or cardinal climber. Good perennial vines include trumpet creeper, English ivy, and winter creeper. You can put your climbers in the ground or select a variety that thrives in planters or pots. Be sure, however, that the plants you choose are well-suited to the light exposure they'll receive.

TOOLS & MATERIALS

- Tape measure
- Posthole digger
- Level
- Drill
- Mason's string
- Reciprocating saw
- Wheelbarrow
- Trowel
- Hammer
- Wood sealer
- Compactible gravel
- Quick-setting concrete mix
- 8 ft. cedar 4 × 4s (2)
- Scrap 2 × 4s
- Deck post finials (2)
- 2 × 3 fence brackets (4)
- 1½" sheet metal screws
- 8 ft. cedar 2 × 4s (2)
- 1" pan-head sheet metal screws
- 1½" screw eyes
- Plastic-coated wire
- Galvanized finish nails

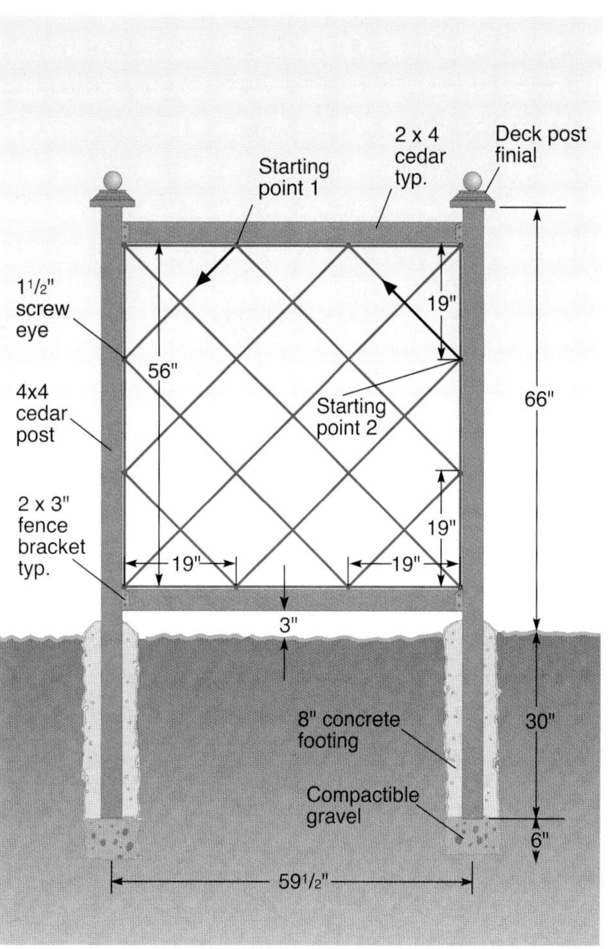

HOW TO BUILD A POST & WIRE TRELLIS

Step A: Prepare & Set the Posts

1. Apply a wood sealer to the bottom 2½" ft. of each post and let dry. For extra protection, let the bottom of the post soak in wood sealer overnight.

2. At the chosen site, mark the posthole locations by setting two wooden stakes in the ground, 59½" apart.

3. Dig the postholes 36" deep. Doing this job properly requires a posthole digger or power auger. Put a 6" layer of compactible gravel in the bottom of each posthole.

4. Set the first post into a hole. Take a carpenter's level and make sure the the post is plumb on two

***A.** Dig two 36"-deep postholes, and then add a 6" layer of gravel to each. Set a post into each hole, and align it. When it's plumb, use 2 × 4s to brace the post in position.*

***B.** Pour quick-setting concrete into the postholes, adding concrete until it's slightly above ground level. Form the wet concrete into a gentle mound around the base of the post.*

adjacent sides.

5. When the post is plumb, use stakes and scrap pieces of 2 × 4 to brace it in position. Repeat the process for the other post.

6. When both posts are plumb and braced, use a mason's string to make certain the tops and sides are aligned. Adjust as necessary.

C. *On top of each post, set a decorative deck finial. Drill pilot holes and secure the finials with small galvanized finish nails.*

Step B: Pour the Footings

1. Following the manufacturer's instructions, mix quick-setting concrete in a wheelbarrow. Mix only enough for one post—quick-setting concrete sets in about 15 minutes.

2. Pour the concrete into one posthole, until the concrete is slightly above ground level.

3. Check the post one more time to make sure it's plumb and properly aligned.

4. With a trowel, form the wet concrete into a gentle mound around the base of the post.

5. Repeat the process for the other post, taking care that it's plumb and aligned with the first post.

6. Let the concrete set for one to two hours.

Step C: Install the Finials

1. Check the tops of the posts to make sure they're level. If not, use a reciprocating saw to trim one post until it's level with the other.

2. Set a decorative deckpost finial on top of each post. Drill two pilot holes on each side and secure the finials with galvanized nails.

Step D: Install Stringers & Screw Eyes

1. Attach the bottom 2 × 3 fence brackets with 1½" pan-head sheet metal screws, 3" above the bottom of each post.

2. To make the stringers, measure the distance between brackets and cut two cedar 2 × 4s to length. Insert one 2 × 4 in the bottom set of brackets and attach it with 1" pan-head sheet metal screws.

D. *Attach the fence brackets 3" from the bottoms of the posts, using sheet metal screws.*

E. *Run wire diagonally between the screw eyes on the posts and stringers.*

3. Measure 56" up from the top of the first stringer. Install top brackets and fasten the second 2 × 4 to the top set of brackets.

Step E: String the Wire

1. Starting in one corner where a stringer meets a post, make a mark on the inside edge of the stringer, 19" from the corner. Next, mark the inside face of the post, 19" from the corner. Repeat the process for the remaining three corners.

2. Drill pilot holes and attach screw eyes at each of the marked points. At the corners, angle the pilot holes at 45° toward the center of the trellis frame.

3. Using plastic-coated wire or clothesline, begin putting the trellis together by knotting the wire on the screw eye at the marked starting point. Feed it through the closest screw eye on the post and down through the screw eye below that. Following the diagram on page 79, continue stringing the wire in a diagonal, back and forth pattern, finishing at the lower screw eye on the opposite post.

4. Beginning at the second starting point (as indicated on the diagram on page 79), string a second wire. Thread it as described above to complete the opposing diagonal runs.

VARIATION: SIMPLE TRELLIS PLAN

1. You can build an easier, less decorative version of the Post & Wire Trellis without the stringers and the crosshatch wire layout. Start by following the directions for Steps A through C.

2. Measuring 1" from the inside tops of the posts, mark the location of the first screw eye. Then continue marking screw eye locations every 8" down the post, putting the last mark a few inches off the ground. Repeat the process for the other post.

3. Drill pilot holes and install the screw eyes, twisting them so that the "eyes" are parallel to the ground, not at right angles to it.

4. Attach the plastic-coated wire with a secure knot to one of the top screw eyes. Then feed the wire through the screw eye on the opposite side, then down through the screw eye directly below.

5. Pull the wire across to the second screw eye down on the opposite side, feeding it through and down to the screw eye directly below. Keep the wire as taut as possible at every run.

6. Continue this process until you reach the final screw eye, and then knot the wire securely.

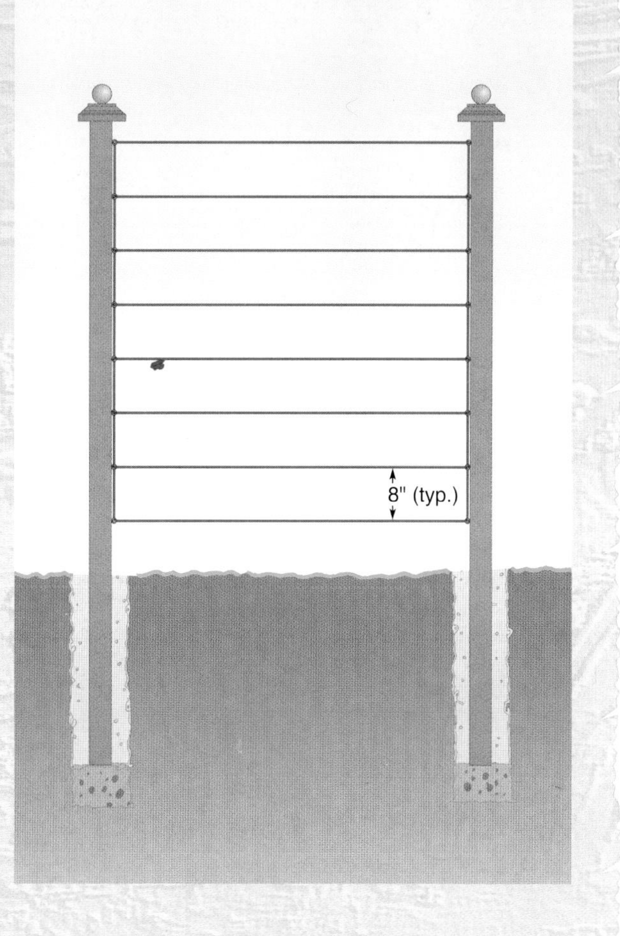

HANGING BASKETS ADDITION

1. To make use of the outside or front edge of the posts, install decorative brackets for hanging plants. Position brackets along the side or front of the post as desired, centered along the post. Mark the screw holes and drill pilot holes. Each post should accommodate at least two brackets.

2. Attach brackets with the screws supplied, and hang planter baskets.

Copper Trellises

Building garden ornaments from copper plumbing materials is just plain fun. And the results are impressive, despite the fact that the pieces are as easy to put together as children's construction toys. Even mastering the technique of soldering (see page 101) is simple, especially since the joints don't have to be watertight.

Plumbing materials are meant to be exposed to water, heat, and cold, so copper ornaments are naturally weather-resistant. To my eye, their appearance actually improves as the bright glow of new copper gives way to the rich patina of older pieces. If you prefer the look of bright copper, spray the finished piece with a clear acrylic sealer to help maintain its color.

As building materials go, copper is quite reasonably priced. Amazingly enough, you can build either of these trellises for well under $100, a fraction of the price of similar pieces featured in many catalogs and stores.

Copper plumbing materials are available at many hardware stores and virtually every home center. However, the arch project on page 86 employs two brass cross fittings that aren't as widely available. You may have to order them through a plumbing supply house, but it should take only a phone call or two to locate a source. The model we used is a #735 ½" sweat cross manufactured by NIBCO.

If you haven't worked with copper before, you'll probably want to start by following these directions exactly. Once you're comfortable with the basic techniques, you can tailor the design to the style of your garden and the location you have in mind. Remember that if an idea doesn't work, the materials aren't wasted: Just reheat the solder, pop off the fittings, and start again.

TOOLS & MATERIALS

- Drill
- Tape measure
- Tubing cutter
- Propane torch
- Jig saw
- Hand maul
- Plywood scraps
- 6" to 8" pieces of ⅜" dowel (4)
- Wood glue
- ½" copper pipe (25 ft.)
- ½"copper tees (16)
- ½" copper 90° elbows (4)
- ½" flexible copper tubing
- Solder
- Flux
- Flux brush
- Nylon scouring pad
- Wire brush
- 3 ft. sections of #3 rebar (2)

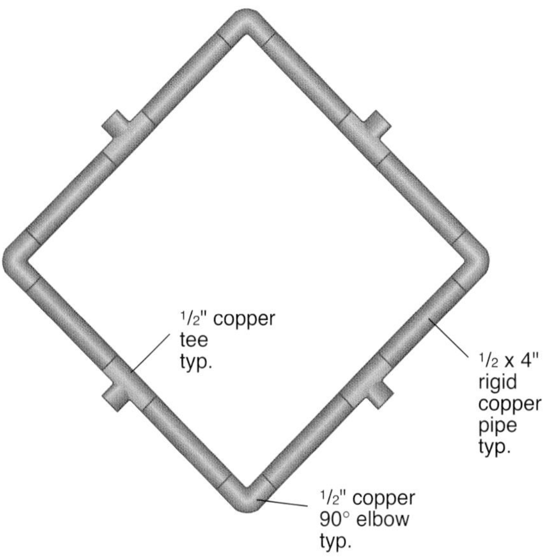

CROWN DETAIL

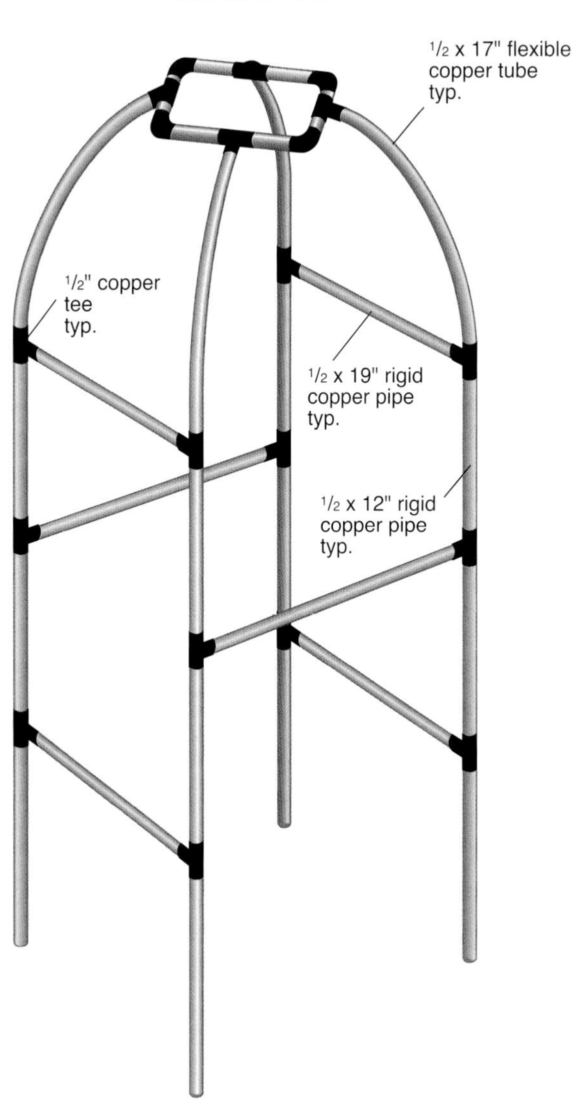

HOW TO BUILD A SQUARE COPPER TRELLIS

Step A: Build a Support Jig

It can be difficult to balance the growing structure of a trellis while it's being dry-fitted, and during the soldering process the pipe gets too hot to handle. The simple solution is to build a jig to support the trellis as you're building it.

Mark a 20" square on a scrap of plywood. Drill a ⅜" hole at each corner, and glue a 6"- to 8"-long dowel into each hole. As you build the trellis, slide the pipes over the dowels.

Step B: Cut the Pipe

1. Measure and mark the copper pipe, following the cutting list shown below.

2. Cut the copper pipe to length. The best way to cut either rigid or flexible copper pipe is with a tubing cutter (page 100). You can cut copper pipe with a hacksaw, but it's more difficult to make straight cuts, and straight cuts make it much easier to solder the joints.

Step C: Assemble the Base

1. Clean and flux the pipes for the base (see page

CUTTING LIST

½" Rigid Copper Pipe

Quantity	Length
12	12"
6	19"
8	4"

½" Flexible Copper Tubing

Quantity	Length
4	17"

VARIATION: COPPER ARCH

TOOLS & MATERIALS

- Drill
- Tape measure
- Tubing cutter or hacksaw
- Round file (optional)
- Propane torch
- Plywood scraps, at least 10 × 60" (2)
- 6" to 8" pieces of 3/8" dowel (6)
- 1 × 2s, at least 46" long (3)
- 1" deck screws (12)
- Wood glue
- 1/2" copper pipe (80 ft.)
- 1/2" copper tees (24)
- 1/2" copper 45° elbows (6)
- 1/2" copper 90° elbows (3)
- 1/2" sweat crosses (2)
- Solder
- Flux
- Flux brush
- Emery cloth or nylon scouring pad
- Wire brush
- 30" sections of #3 rebar (6)
- Hand maul

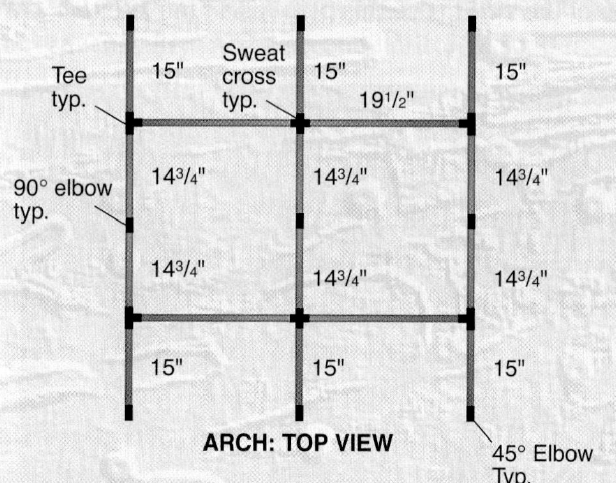

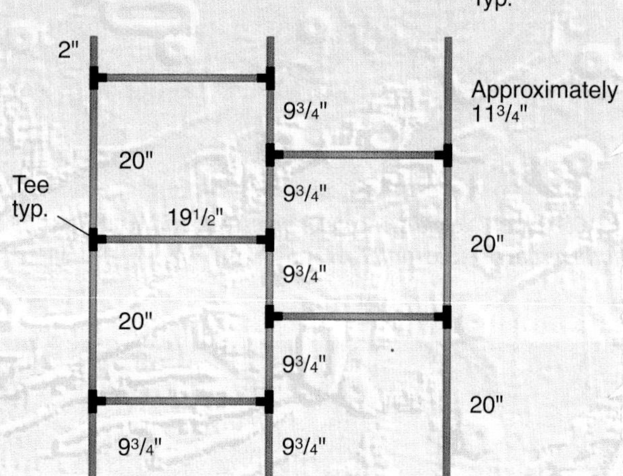

CUTTING LIST

1/2" Copper Pipe

Quantity	Length
8	20"
14	19 1/2"
12	9 3/4"
6	15"
6	14 3/4"
2	14"
4	2"

HOW TO BUILD A COPPER ARCH

Step A: Cut the Pipe & Build a Support Jig

1. Measure, mark, and cut the copper pipe, following the cutting list shown at right below. Clean and flux the pipes (page 100).

2. To build a support jig, start with two scraps of plywood at least 10" wide and 60" long. Down the center of each piece, draw a 40" line, and then drill three 3/8" holes, placed at 20" intervals along the line. Glue a 6" to 8" piece of dowel in each hole. On each of three 1 × 2s, draw a pair of marks 42 1/2" apart. Lay the 1 × 2s across the pieces of plywood, aligning the marks on the 1 × 2s with the lines on the plywood to set the exact spacing for the sides of the arch. Secure the

A. *Make two supports by gluing dowels at 20" intervals to scraps of plywood. On three 1 × 2s, make marks 42 1/2" apart. Align the marks and screw the 1 × 2s to the plywood supports.*

pieces carefully.

Step E: Build the Crown & Assemble the Trellis

1. Dry-fit one 17" length of ½" flexible copper tubing between the base and the crown. Bend the copper so that the crown will sit level and square at the top of the trellis. Use this piece as a template to

***D.** Combine 4" lengths of copper pipe, tees, and 90° elbows to form a square piece for the crown.*

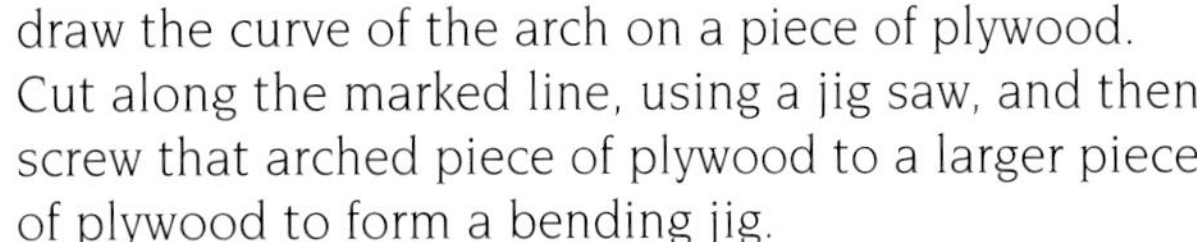

draw the curve of the arch on a piece of plywood. Cut along the marked line, using a jig saw, and then screw that arched piece of plywood to a larger piece of plywood to form a bending jig.

2. Bend the three remaining pieces of flexible copper tubing by simply shaping each one around the bending jig.

3. Assemble the arched pieces of the dome and the crown, and then fit this assembly on the base. Make sure the arches are equally curved and positioned symmetrically, and that the crown is level and square within the trellis. Adjust as necessary.

4. Solder the joints of the crown and dome, then the joints attaching the dome to the base.

5. When the solder on the joints has lost its shiny color, clean excess solder and flux from each joint, using a nylon pad.

Step F: Install the Trellis

1. Select a site for your trellis, and mark a 20" square on the ground, tracing it on the soil or making the lines with a trail of flour.

2. At two opposite corners of the marked square, drive a 3 ft. piece of rebar about 18" into the ground. (Caution: buried utility lines are dangerous. Always call your utility providers before digging any holes or driving anything deep into the soil.)

3. Fit two legs of the trellis over the buried rebar, firmly anchoring it in place.

***E.** Dry-fit one arch of the dome, and then use that piece to create a bending jig for the remaining pieces of the dome.*

***F.** Mark a 20" square on the ground, and drive pieces of rebar at two of the corners, 18" deep. Position the trellis over the rebar.*

VARIATION: COPPER ARCH

TOOLS & MATERIALS

- Drill
- Tape measure
- Tubing cutter or hacksaw
- Round file (optional)
- Propane torch
- Plywood scraps, at least 10 × 60" (2)
- 6" to 8" pieces of ⅜" dowel (6)
- 1 × 2s, at least 46" long (3)
- 1" deck screws (12)
- Wood glue
- ½" copper pipe (80 ft.)
- ½" copper tees (24)
- ½" copper 45° elbows (6)
- ½" copper 90° elbows (3)
- ½" sweat crosses (2)
- Solder
- Flux
- Flux brush
- Emery cloth or nylon scouring pad
- Wire brush
- 30" sections of #3 rebar (6)
- Hand maul

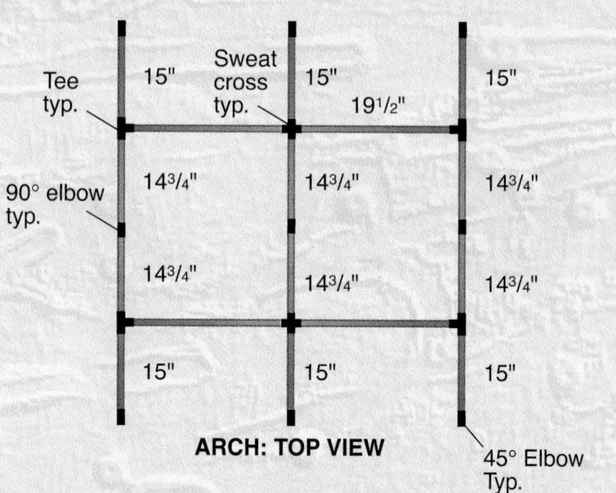

ARCH: TOP VIEW

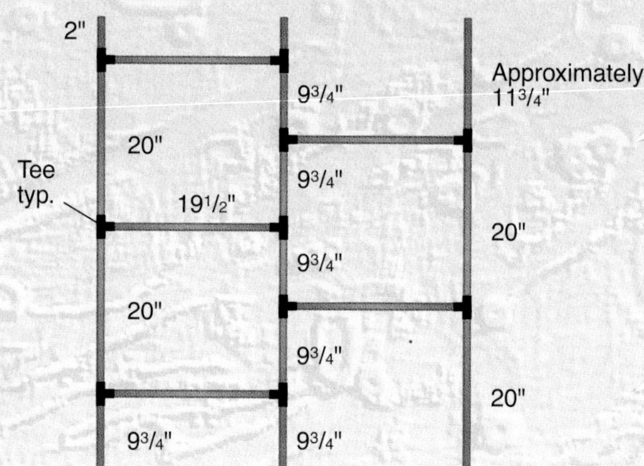

LEG ASSEMBLY: SIDE VIEW

HOW TO BUILD A COPPER ARCH

Step A: Cut the Pipe & Build a Support Jig

1. Measure, mark, and cut the copper pipe, following the cutting list shown at right below. Clean and flux the pipes (page 100).

2. To build a support jig, start with two scraps of plywood at least 10" wide and 60" long. Down the center of each piece, draw a 40" line, and then drill three ⅜" holes, placed at 20" intervals along the line. Glue a 6" to 8" piece of dowel in each hole. On each of three 1 × 2s, draw a pair of marks 42½" apart. Lay the 1 × 2s across the pieces of plywood, aligning the marks on the 1 × 2s with the lines on the plywood to set the exact spacing for the sides of the arch. Secure the

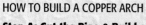

***A.** Make two supports by gluing dowels at 20" intervals to scraps of plywood. On three 1 × 2s, make marks 42½" apart. Align the marks and screw the 1 × 2s to the plywood supports.*

CUTTING LIST

½" Copper Pipe

Quantity	Length
8	20"
14	19½"
12	9¾"
6	15"
6	14¾"
2	14"
4	2"

B. *Dry-fit the entire leg assembly, alternating pipe and tees to form the legs, and adding horizontal supports in between.*

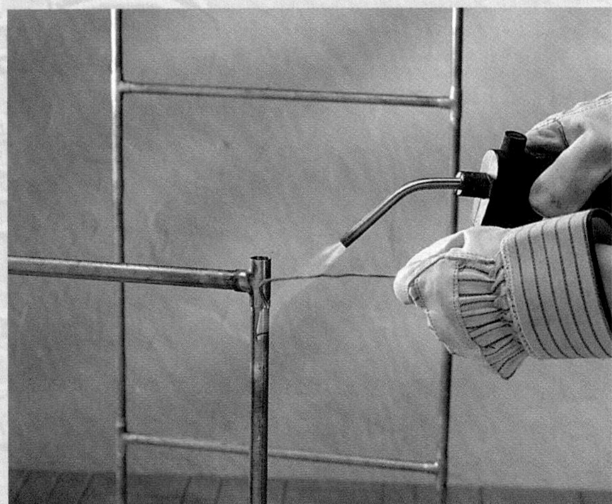

C. *Disassemble the pieces and solder each joint, working from the ground up.*

1 × 2s to the plywood, using 1" screws.

Step B: Construct the Leg Assemblies

1. Slide a 9¾" length of pipe over the first dowel, add a tee; then alternate pipe and tees as indicated on the drawing on page 86.

2. Slide a 9¾" length of pipe over the second dowel, and then alternate tees and pipe as indicated.

3. Fit 19½" lengths of pipe between pairs of tees to form horizontal supports.

4. Slide a 20" length of pipe over the third dowel, and then alternate tees and 20" lengths as indicated. To make sure the arch remains square, cut the final piece in place: Add a 14" piece of pipe, and then use a level to mark and cut it to match the first two legs (it should measure approximately 11¾").

5. Fit 19½" pieces of pipe between the remaining pairs of tees, creating horizontal supports.

6. Repeat numbers 1 through 5 to construct a leg assembly for the other side.

Step C: Solder the Leg Assemblies

Disassemble the pieces and solder the joints in each leg assembly, working from the ground up. When the joints are cool, set the assemblies aside.

Step D: Construct the Arch

1. Working on a flat surface, connect two 14¾" lengths of pipe, using a 90° elbow. Add a tee, then a 15" length of pipe to each side. Repeat to form a second, identical arch.

2. To form the center arch, connect two 14¾" lengths of pipe, using a 90° elbow. Add a sweat cross and a 15" piece of pipe to each side.

D. *Using 90° elbows, pipe, and tees, build three arch assemblies. Connect the arches with horizontal braces, tees, and crosses.*

3. Slide a 45° elbow onto each dowel of the support jig, and then slide the legs of the arches into those elbows.

4. Add 19½" lengths of pipe between sets of tees and crosses, forming horizontal supports as indicated on page 86.

5. Disassemble the pieces, and rebuild the arch assembly, soldering as you go. When the joints are cool, set the assembly aside.

6. Put the leg assemblies back onto the support jig, and fit the arch assembly in place and solder the joints.

7. Follow Step F, page 85, to install the arch in the garden.

Rustic Arbor

Truly successful gardens reflect the architectural style of the surrounding buildings as well as the shape of the terrain and the personality of the gardener. Some settings call for formal accessories and manicured plantings; others call for contemporary forms, while still others require informal arrangements and accessories. A large piece, such as this rustic arbor, can set the tone for a garden or help reinforce an established theme.

This arbor would harmonize beautifully with any landscape that calls for a natural, unstructured form. In a woodland setting, you can take advantage of the fact that most of the materials are free for the cutting. Even in a city, it shouldn't be hard to come by the branches you need. We cut ours at a suburban construction site—with the permission of the builder, of course. Although we gathered vines for the decorative accents from the woods, it might be easier to buy grapevines, which are available at most craft stores.

Cut the straightest branches you can find, but don't worry if some of them are slightly bent or misshapen. Position the branches to maintain the basic dimensions, and consider any variations to be artistic character.

Although a rustic arbor is simple to construct, it's much easier with two people. Lashing pieces in place simplifies the process of securing the braces, but maneuvering the crosspieces into position is definitely a job for two.

TOOLS & MATERIALS

- Tape measure
- Loppers
- Jig saw
- Scrub brush
- Drill
- Aviation snips
- Hammer
- Stapler
- Shovel
- Whiskey barrel halves (2)
- Horticultural disinfectant
- Exterior wood sealer
- Washed pea gravel
- Zinc gauze or tight wire mesh, at least 1 ft. × 1 ft.
- Freshly cut 1½"-dia. branches
- Flexible vines, such as grapevines
- 2½" galvanized deck screws
- 1½" galvanized brads
- Raffia or natural twine
- Large rocks (4 to 6)
- Potting soil
- Climbing vines

HOW TO BUILD A RUSTIC ARBOR

Step A: Gather & Prepare the Branches

1. Cut a supply of branches 1½" in diameter, lopping them off at approximately the following lengths: four branches 9 ft. long (for the uprights); two branches 7 to 8 ft. long (for the crosspieces); an assortment that produces four 4½ ft. pieces (for the diagonal supports); and an assortment that produces ten 2 ft. pieces (for the braces). Also, cut the vines into eight 46" pieces.

2. Remove any twigs and small branches, using loppers. Cut the pieces to size, using a jig saw to

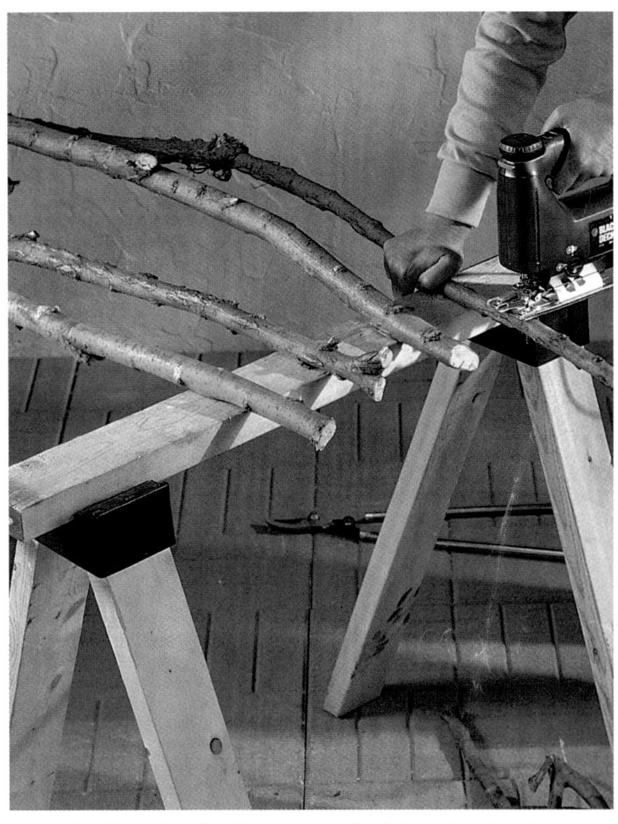

A. *Gather branches for the framework of the arbor. Cut the branches to size and seal the ends with exterior wood sealer.*

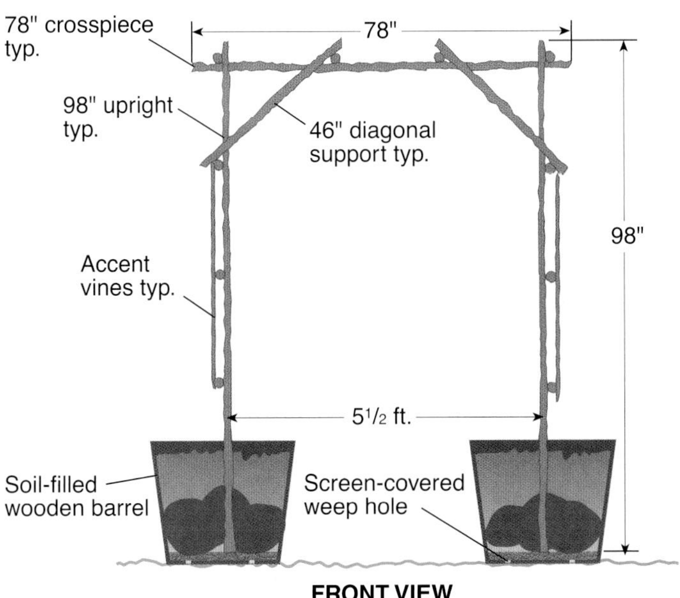

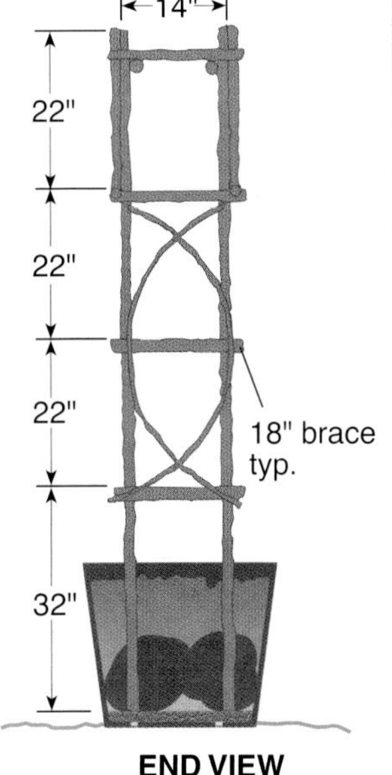

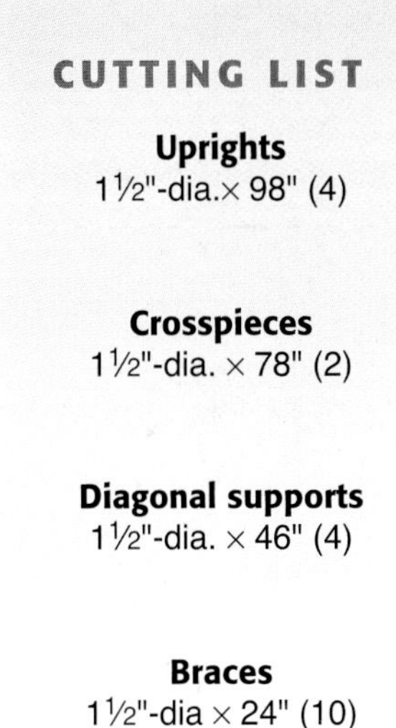

CUTTING LIST

Uprights
1½"-dia.× 98" (4)

Crosspieces
1½"-dia. × 78" (2)

Diagonal supports
1½"-dia. × 46" (4)

Braces
1½"-dia × 24" (10)

make each cut as square as possible.

3. Apply exterior wood sealer to each branch, particularly the cut ends. Allow the branches to dry.

Step B: Prepare the Barrels

1. Select two half-size whiskey barrels to anchor the arbor. Prod the surfaces of the barrels, especially the corners and bottoms, with a knife to make sure they're sound and free of rot.

2. Fill the barrels with water and let them soak for several hours. Scrub each barrel inside and out with

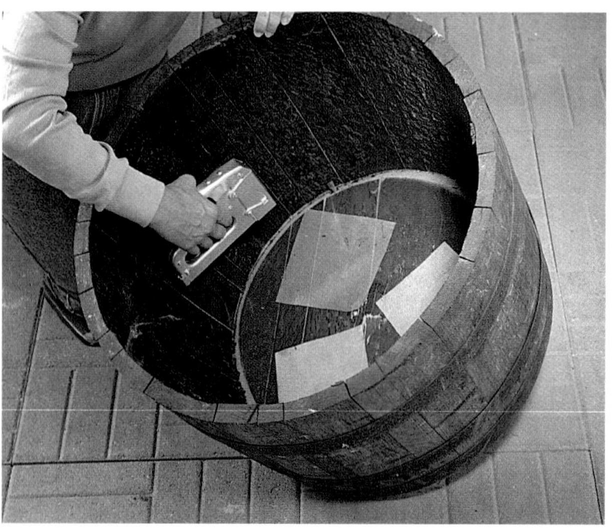

B. *Scrub and disinfect two whiskey barrels, and then drill weep holes in the bottom of each. Seal the interiors, staple mesh over the weep holes, and add a 2" layer of gravel.*

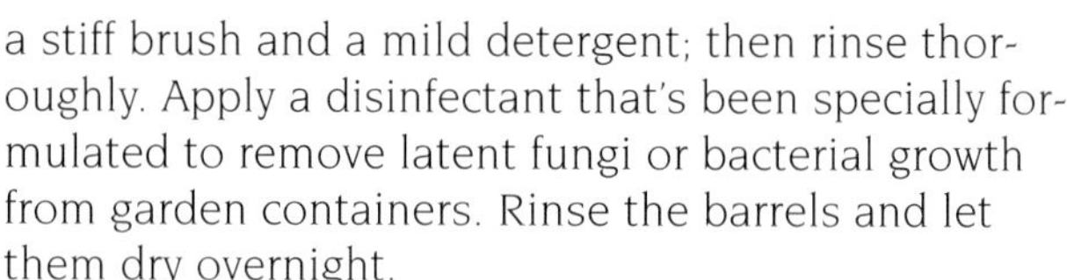

a stiff brush and a mild detergent; then rinse thoroughly. Apply a disinfectant that's been specially formulated to remove latent fungi or bacterial growth from garden containers. Rinse the barrels and let them dry overnight.

3. Drill three or four 3⁄8" weep holes in the bottom of each barrel.

4. Apply a coat of exterior wood sealer to the interior of each barrel, making sure the raw edges of the drainage holes are coated. Let the sealer dry.

5. Using aviation snips, cut small squares of zinc gauze and then staple one over each drainage hole. Add a 2" layer of washed pea gravel to the bottom of each barrel.

Step C: Build the Framework

1. Lay out two uprights on a work surface, positioning them parallel to one another and 14" apart. Measure the distance between the uprights and adjust them until they are roughly parallel, given the natural shape of the branches.

2. Position an 18" branch across a pair of uprights, 32" from the bottom ends and centered horizontally. Holding this brace firmly in place, drill pilot holes through each end and into the uprights. Secure each joint with a 2½" deck screw. Add another brace every 22" along the uprights, ending with one 2" from the top ends. Repeat this process to construct the other pair of uprights.

3. Follow the general procedures in numbers 1 and 2 to form the crosspiece. Beginning and ending 6"

C. *Arrange uprights parallel to one another and 14" apart on center. Position 18" branches as braces, placing one every 22". Drill pilot holes and secure the joints with 2½" deck screws.*

D. *Position one pair of uprights in each barrel and add soil, tamping the soil around the uprights to hold them in place.*

E. *Lash a diagonal support across each corner of the arbor. Drill pilot holes and secure the diagonal supports to the uprights, using 2½" deck screws.*

F. *Test-fit, mark, and cut vines for the decorative accents. Drill pilot holes and secure the branches to the uprights, using 1½" galvanized brads.*

from the ends, position one brace every 22" along the crosspiece.

Step D: Assemble the Framework

1. Put the barrels in place, positioning them 5½ ft. on center from one another. Set a pair of uprights into one of the barrels and have a helper support them while you prop them in place with several large rocks. Add potting soil, tamping it firmly around the uprights to hold them in place. Continue adding soil to within 2" of the top of the barrel. Repeat the process to install the other pair of uprights.

2. Lift the crosspiece into place, centering it between the uprights. Holding the crosspiece firmly in place, drill pilot holes through each end and into the uprights. Secure each joint with a 2½" deck screw.

Step E: Add Diagonal Supports

1. Lash a diagonal support in place on each side of each corner of the arbor, using raffia or twine. Position these supports to reach from the third brace of the uprights to the first brace of the crosspiece (see diagram, page 89).

2. Drill pilot holes and drive 2½" deck screws through the supports and into the uprights and crosspieces.

Step F: Add the Accents

1. Test-fit a vine for the decorative accents, curving it from the inside edge of the first brace, across the upright to the opposite side of the next brace and then up to the third brace on the original side (see diagram, page 89). Mark and cut the vine to length, then lash it in place.

2. Drill pilot holes and secure the vine in place, using 1½" galvanized brads. Add a vine in the opposite direction, and then repeat the process on the other set of uprights.

3. Secure the vines at the intersections by tying them with raffia or twine.

4. Plant vines in the barrels, placing one plant on each side of each pair of uprights. As they grow, train the vines to grow up and over the arbor.

TIP: EASY TIES

Tying vines requires a material that's both strong and gentle—strong enough to support the vine and gentle enough not to damage the tendrils.

Old 100 percent cotton t-shirts make terrific, inexpensive ties that can go into the compost bin for further recycling after the growing season is over.

Starting at the bottom, cut around the shirt in a continuous spiral about 1½" wide. When you reach the armholes, begin making straight cuts from the edge of one sleeve to the other. One shirt usually produces 15 to 20 yards of tying material.

Brick Pillars

Nothing gives your garden a greater sense of permanence and substance than well-planned and well-executed masonry work. It makes the impression that your garden will be there for decades, not just a few summers. And masonry doesn't have to mean just simple projects like walking paths or borders around your plantings. If you're feeling ambitious, you can tackle a bit of bricklaying.

As masonry projects go, this one is fairly simple. Even if you're a beginner, you can build these elegant, professional-looking pillars if you proceed slowly and follow the instructions carefully. Of course, if you have a friend or relative who knows his (or her) way around brick and mortar, it can't hurt to have an experienced eye check out your progress. (See pages 104 to 107 for additional information on building with bricks.)

Your adventure in bricklaying begins with choosing a site for the pillars and pouring footings to support them. These below-grade columns of concrete provide a stable foundation that will protect your pillars when freezes and thaws cause the soil to shift.

The finished pillars can serve many functions. They can support a gate, frame a flower bed of which you're particularly proud, or support meandering vines. Whatever their primary purpose, you'll enjoy them for years, perhaps decades, as they weather and gain character. And you'll be proud to tell everyone that *you* built them.

TOOLS & MATERIALS

- Mason's string
- Shovel
- Wheelbarrow
- Pencil
- Masonry trowel
- Level
- Jointer
- Tape measure
- Circular saw
- Hand maul
- Rope
- Stakes
- 2 × 4s
- 2 × 2
- 1 × 2
- Concrete mix
- Standard modular bricks (4 × 2⅔ × 8")
- Type N mortar mix
- Small dowel
- Vegetable oil
- ½" wire mesh
- 2 capstones
- ⅜" plywood scraps
- 2½" deck or wallboard screws
- ⅜"-thick wood scraps

A. *Mark the site with stakes and mason's strings; then remove the sod and dig a hole for each footing.*

HOW TO BUILD BRICK PILLARS

Step A: Select & Prepare the Site

1. Select the area in the garden where the pillars are to stand, keeping in mind their rectangular shape and a preferred alignment—long sides or short sides facing out.

2. Make a rough outline of each footing, using a rope. Then lay out a 16 × 20" footing for each pillar, using stakes and mason's strings.

3. Strip away any sod or plant material up to 6" outside the mason's strings on all sides.

4. Dig a hole for each footing to the depth required by local building codes, using the mason's strings as guides. (The required depth depends on the depth of the frost line in your region.) A thin, narrow shovel works well for digging a square hole.

5. Following the layout of the stakes and strings, construct 16 × 20" forms (interior dimensions) for the concrete, using 2 × 4s and screws.

6. Sink the forms into the ground slightly just around the hole so the visible portions of the footings will look neat and provide a flat, even surface for laying bricks.

7. Drive stakes outside the 2 × 4s so the forms are firmly supported. Then adjust the forms until they're level and square.

Step B: Pour the Concrete

1. In a wheelbarrow, mix the dry concrete with water, following the manufacturer's instructions.

2. Pour the concrete into one footing hole, filling it to the top of the form.

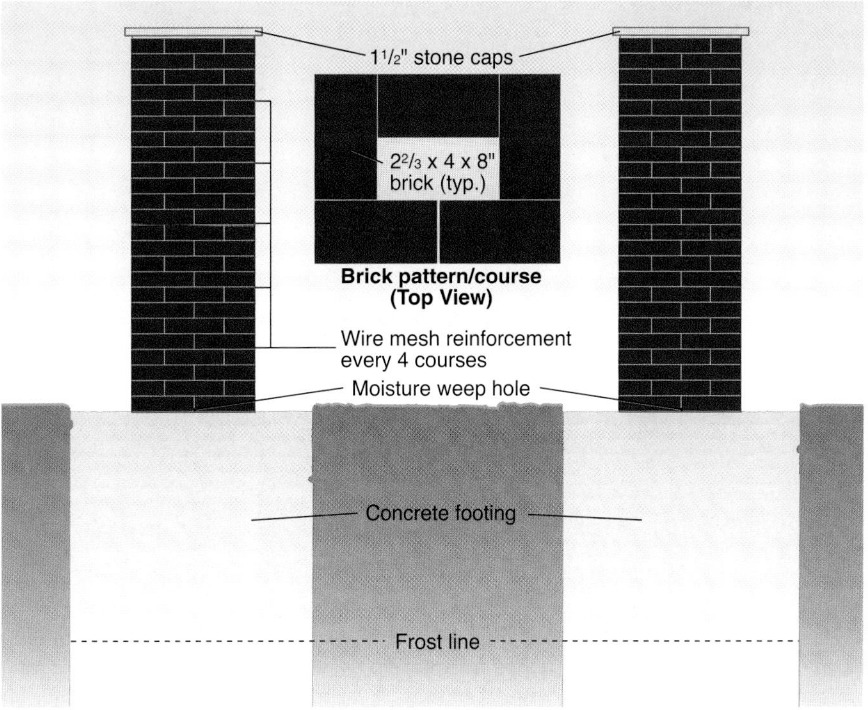

3. Drag a scrap 2 × 4 across the top of the form, "screeding" away any excess concrete. The surface of the footing should be smooth and even.

4. Repeat the process for the other footing, and then clean the wheelbarrow thoroughly with a hose.

5. Let the concrete cure for at least two days before removing the forms and building on top of the footings. Waiting a week is even better.

Step C: Build a Story Pole

1. As you build the pillars, a story pole allows you to check the positions of the courses of brick and the thickness of the mortar joints. To build a story pole, start by cutting a batch of spacers from ⅜" plywood.

2. On a wide, flat surface, lay out ten or more courses of brick. With the bricks lying on their sides, insert spacers between each pair, making sure the bricks are spaced ⅜" apart.

3. Place a straight 1 × 2 alongside the bricks; then mark the space between each pair of bricks, indicating the intended location and thickness of each layer of mortar.

Step D: Dry-Lay the Bricks

1. After the footings have cured, arrange five of the bricks to form a rectangle on one of the footings.

2. Insert spacers between the bricks to establish the thickness of the vertical mortar joints. Take care that the bricks are correctly centered on each footing and square in relation to each other.

3. With a grease pencil or carpenter's pencil, draw reference lines on the footing around the bricks.

Step E: Lay the First Course

1. Prepare the mortar, according to the instructions on the bag.

2. Using a trowel, lay a bed of mortar within the reference lines to a thickness of about ⅜", forming the mortar into a rectangle.

3. Apply ⅜" of mortar to the sides of alternating bricks, so that mortar fills the spaces between them, and set the bricks on the mortar bed, tapping each one gently with the handle of the trowel.

B. *In order to create a smooth, level surface, drag a 2 × 4 across the top of the form, removing any excess concrete.*

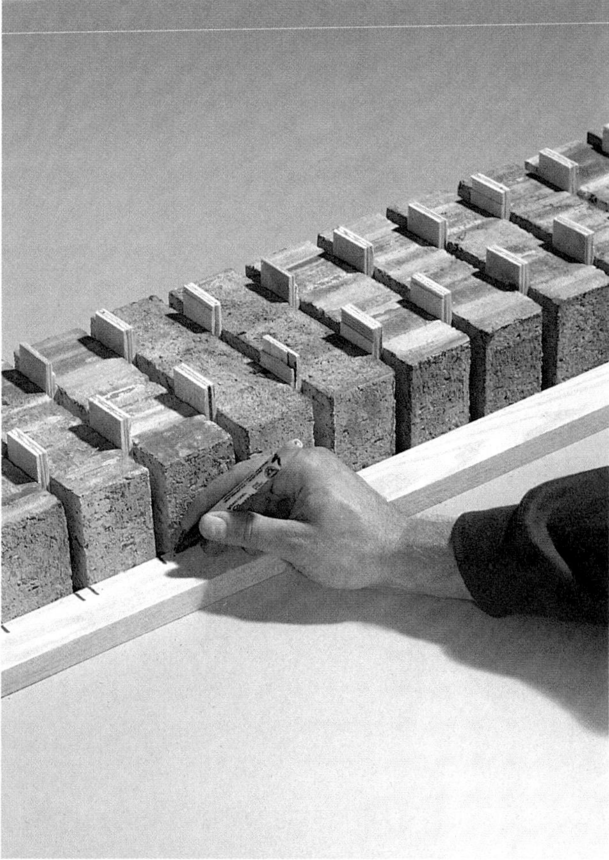

C. *With the 1 × 2 lying beside the arranged bricks, mark the ⅜" spaces between the bricks to create a story pole.*

4. On the side of the pillar that's seen least often, use a small wooden dowel or pencil coated with vegetable oil to make a weep hole in the wet mortar between two bricks. (This weep hole helps ensure proper drainage of any moisture that accumulates inside the pillar.)

5. When all five bricks in the first course are laid, make sure they're square and level. If necessary, adjust bricks by gently tapping them with the handle of the trowel.

Step F: Lay the Second Course

1. Apply mortar to the top of the first course of bricks, again 3/8" thick.

2. Lay the second course of brick in the mortar, but rotate the pattern 180°. Gently remove the oiled dowel or pencil from the mortar of the first course.

3. Check the pillar with a level, making sure your work is both level and plumb. Gently adjust bricks as necessary. Then, use the story pole as a guide to make sure the two courses on all sides are correctly spaced. Small errors made low on the pillar will be exaggerated with each successive course. Check your work after every two courses of brick.

Step G: Add Wire Mesh

1. Proceed with the next two courses and apply mortar to the top of the fourth course. Then cut a piece of 1/4" wire mesh slightly smaller than the dimensions of a course of bricks, and lay it into the mortar for lateral reinforcement. Apply more mortar to the top of the wire mesh, and lay the fifth course of brick.

2. Add wire-mesh reinforcement after every fourth course.

Step H: Tool the Joints & Complete the Pillar

1. After the fifth course, use a jointer to smooth and pack down (a step known as "tooling") the mortar joints below that have hardened enough to resist minimal finger pressure.

2. Continue to lay bricks until the next-to-last course. Remember to check your work with the story

D. *Dry-lay the first course by arranging the bricks as they will be mortared. Draw reference lines around the bricks.*

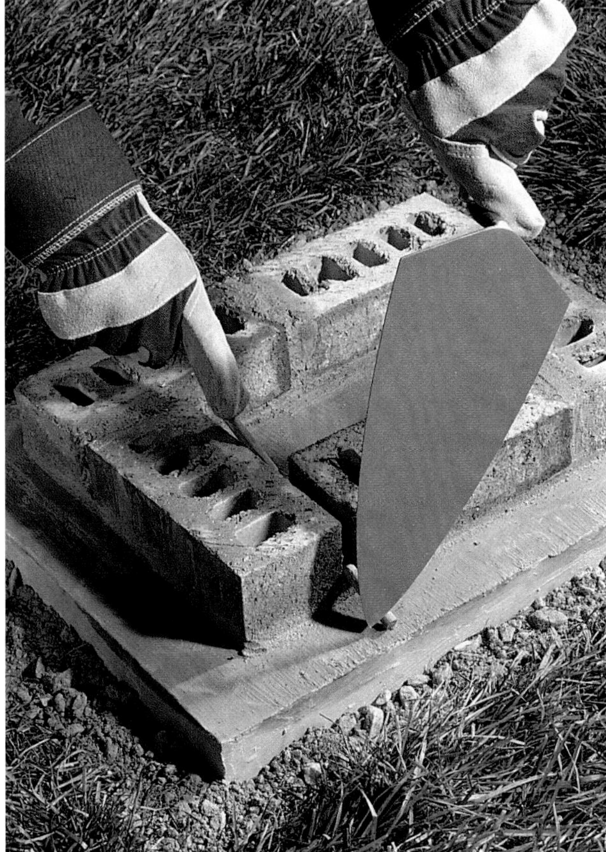

E. *Lay an oiled dowel into the wet mortar, creating a weep hole. Then fill in with mortar above the dowel.*

F. *When laying the second course of bricks, rotate the pattern 180° to add strength and create a more visually pleasing look.*

pole after every two courses, install wire mesh every four courses, and tool the joints as the mortar in each course becomes firm.

3. Apply mortar to the next-to-last course, and add a piece of wire mesh. Apply mortar to the entire surface of the wire mesh.

4. Lay the side of the last course formed by two bricks. Then add an extra brick in the center, over the mortar-covered wire mesh.

5. Lay the remaining bricks so they fit snugly around the center brick.

6. Tool any remaining joints, as soon as they become firm.

Step I: Build the Second Pillar

1. Lay the first course of brick, following the instructions in Steps D and E above. Measure the distance between the pillars with a tape measure.

2. Make a measuring rod by cutting a 2 × 2 or other straight board to match the distance between the bases of the two pillars. Use the rod every few courses to check that the second pillar is aligned with (parallel to) the first. Also, consult the story

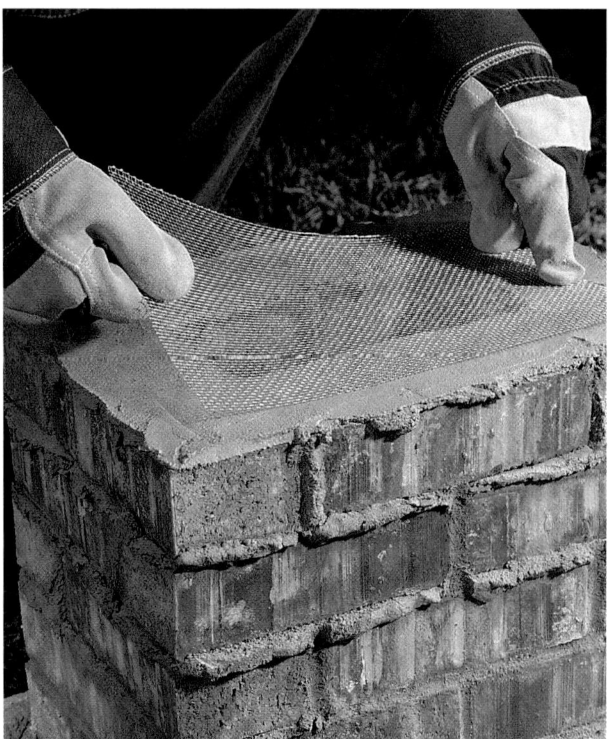

G. *Lay a piece of wire mesh in the wet mortar after every four courses.*

H. *After the fifth course of bricks is laid, use a jointer to tool, or smooth, the mortar joints.*

pole after every two courses.

3. Complete the second pillar, following the instructions in Steps F through H.

Step J: Prepare & Install the Capstones

1. Have a stone supplier in your area cut two capstones so that each one is roughly 1½" longer and wider than the top of the pillars.

2. Draw diagonal reference lines from corner to corner on the bottoms of the capstones. Then, using the dimensions of the pillar and the diagonal lines, draw a rectangle centered on the bottom of each capstone.

3. Apply a ½"-thick bed of mortar to the top of the pillar, and center the capstone on the pillar, using the reference lines. Tool the mortar joint so it's flush with the brick. Note: If mortar begins to squeeze out of the joint, press ⅜"-thick wood scraps into the mortar on each side to support the cap. After 24 hours, use a hammer to tap out the wood scraps, and fill in the spaces with fresh mortar.

VARIATIONS: GARDEN PILLARS

Using these plans, it's possible to create garden pillars with different decorative or functional qualities.

- Build three or four pillars in graduated sizes to create a terraced effect.
- Use pillars as pedestals around the garden to highlight large pots full of cascading blooms or favorite outdoor statuary.
- Visit a masonry supply house or building center and gather ideas on how to use bricks of different colors and textures. You can lay bricks of different shades in alternating courses. For a more subtle effect, alternate same-colored bricks of different textures–smooth, rough, smooth, rough.
- Build short pillars that act as the base of an arbor or outdoor bench.

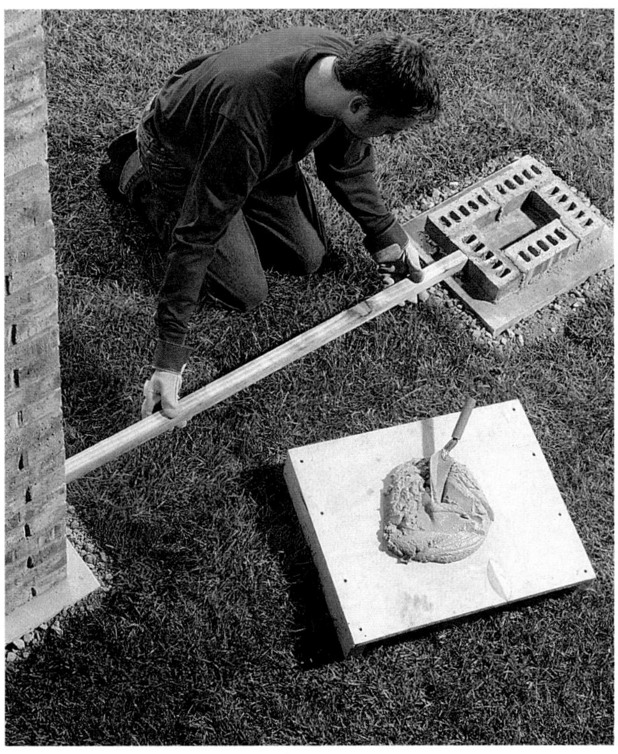

I. *Lay the first course of the second pillar. Measure and cut a 2 × 2 to match the distance between the pillars. As you build the second pillar, use this board to check its alignment.*

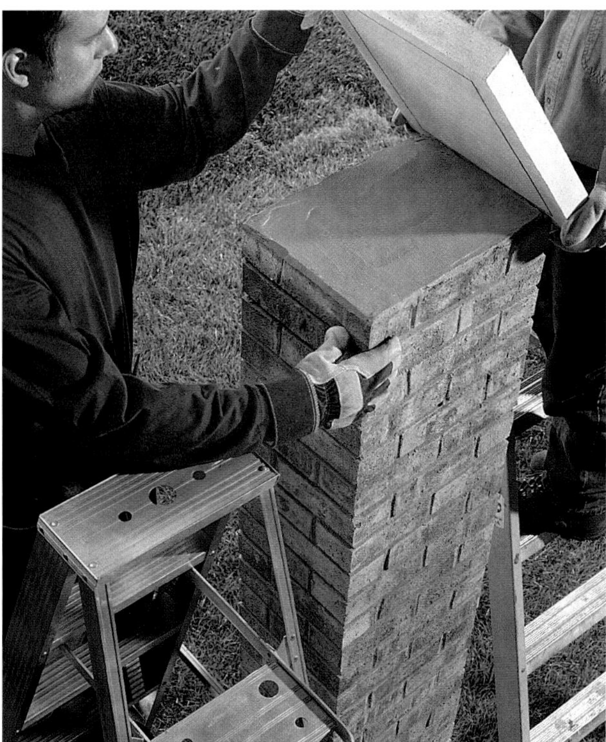

J. *Place mortar on top of the pillar, and set the capstone in position. Strike the mortar joint beneath the capstone flush with the pillar.*

WARNING • BE SAFE • WEAR SAFETY GOGGLES

Basic Techniques

Stop worrying; help is on the way! If any of the projects on the previous pages fill you with dread, you can now relax. While designing the projects for this book, I've made sure to keep them simple enough that just about anyone can complete them.

Still, if a project uses materials or techniques that are new to you, you may need an introduction to some basic skills, whether its fitting copper pipe (pages 100 to 101), mixing masonry materials (pages 102 to 103), splitting bricks (pages 104 to 107), or wiring a GFCI receptacle (pages 108 to 110). Make sure to allow yourself extra time to become familiar with the techniques and materials used in the project you're building, perhaps practicing with scrap materials before you begin. For example, even though I've soldered copper pipe, I still find it reassuring to review the techniques for working with a torch before starting a new pipe-fitting project. And working with hypertufa—that strange mud with the odd name—was a new experience for me altogether. If you find yourself in the same situation, this chapter will give you some useful background information for building the projects in this book.

This chapter is intended as a reference, so don't feel you need to read it from start to finish. You probably have your eye on a project you're planning to build. Select the information you need from this chapter, and start having fun. Later, as you build your third, fourth, or fourteenth project, you can return to these pages to pick up new skills.

IN THIS CHAPTER:

Cutting & Soldering Copper

A soldered pipe joint, also called a sweated joint, is made by heating a copper or brass fitting with a propane torch until the fitting is just hot enough to melt solder. The heat then draws the solder into the gap between the fitting and the copper pipe, forming a strong seal.

Using too much heat is the most common mistake made by beginners. To avoid this error, remember that the tip of the torch's inner flame produces the most heat. Direct the flame carefully—solder will flow in the direction the heat has traveled. Heat the pipe just until the flux sizzles; remove the flame and touch the solder to the pipe. The heated pipe will quickly melt the solder.

Soldering copper pipe and fittings isn't difficult, but it requires some patience and skill. It's a good idea to practice soldering pieces of scrap pipe before taking on a large project.

HOW TO SOLDER COPPER PIPE

Step A: Cut the Pipe

1. Measure and mark the pipe. Place a tubing cutter over the pipe with the cutting wheel centered over the marked line. Tighten the handle until the pipe rests on both rollers.

2. Turn the tubing cutter one rotation to score a continuous line around the pipe. Then rotate the cutter in the other direction. After every two rotations, tighten the handle.

3. Remove metal burrs from the inside edge of the cut pipe, using the reaming point on the tubing cutter or a round file.

Step B: Clean the Pipe & Fittings

To form a good seal with solder, the ends of all pipes and the insides of all fittings must be free of dirt and grease. Sand the ends of pipes with emery cloth, and scour the insides of the fittings with a wire brush.

Step C: Flux & Dry-fit the the Pipes

1. Apply a thin layer of water-soluble paste flux to the end of each pipe, using a flux brush. The flux should cover about 1" of the end of the pipe.

2. Insert the pipe into the fitting until the pipe is tight against the fitting socket, and twist the fitting slightly to spread the flux. If a series of pipes and fittings (a run) is involved, flux and dry-fit the entire run without soldering any of the joints. When you're sure the run is correctly assembled and everything fits, take it apart and prepare to solder the joints.

Step D: Heat the Fittings

1. Shield flammable work surfaces from the heat of the torch. Although heat-absorbent pads are avail-

A. *Position the tubing cutter, and score a line around the pipe. Rotate the cutter until the pipe separates.*

B. *Clean inside the fittings with a wire brush, and deburr the pipes with the reaming point on the tubing cutter.*

C. *Brush a thin layer of flux onto the end of each pipe. Assemble the joint, twisting the fitting to spread the flux.*

able for this purpose, you can use a double layer of 26-gauge sheet metal. The reflective quality of the sheet metal helps joints heat evenly.

2. Unwind 8" to 10" of solder from the spool. To make it easier to maneuver the solder all the way around a joint, bend the first 2" of the wire solder to a 90° angle.

3. Open the gas valve and light the propane torch. Adjust the valve until the inner portion of the flame is 1" to 2" long.

4. Hold the flame tip against the middle of the fitting for 4 to 5 seconds or until the flux begins to sizzle. Heat the other side of the joint, distributing the heat evenly. Move the flame around the joint in the direction the solder should flow. Touch the solder to the pipe, just below the fitting. If it melts, the joint is hot enough.

Step E: Apply the Solder

Quickly apply solder along both seams of the fitting, allowing capillary action to draw the liquefied solder into the fitting. When the joint is filled, solder begins to form droplets on the bottom. A correctly soldered joint shows a thin bead of silver-colored solder around the lip of the fitting. It typically takes about ½" of solder wire to fill a joint in ½" pipe.

If the solder pools around the fitting rather than filling the joint as it cools, reheat the area until the solder liquifies and is drawn in slightly.

Note: *Always turn off the propane torch immediately after you've finished soldering; make sure the gas valve is completely closed.*

Step F: Wipe Away Excess Solder & Check the Joint

1. Let the joint sit undisturbed until the solder loses its shiny color—don't touch it before then—the copper will be quite hot.

2. When the joint is cool enough to touch, wipe away excess flux and solder, using a clean, dry rag. When the joint is completely cool, check for gaps around the edges. If you find gaps, apply more flux to the rim of the joint and resolder it.

3. If, for some reason, you need to take apart a soldered joint, you can reverse the process. First, light the torch and heat the fitting until the solder becomes shiny and begins to melt. Then use channel-type pliers to separate the pipe from the fitting. To remove the old solder, heat the ends of the pipe, and then use a dry rag to carefully wipe away the melted solder. When the pipe is cool, polish the ends down to bare metal, using emery cloth. Discard the old fittings—they can't be reused.

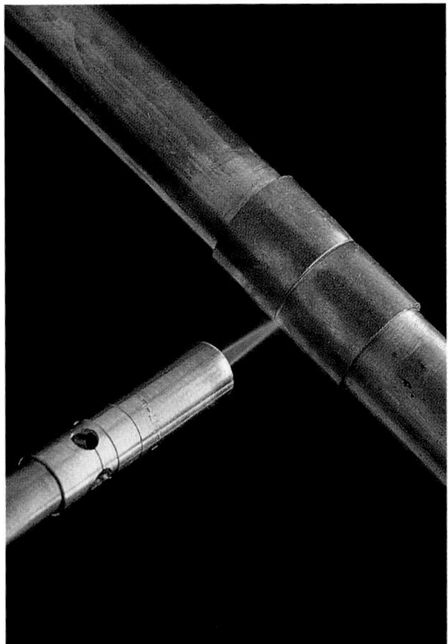

D. *Heat the fitting until the flux begins to sizzle. Concentrate the tip of the torch's flame on the middle of the fitting.*

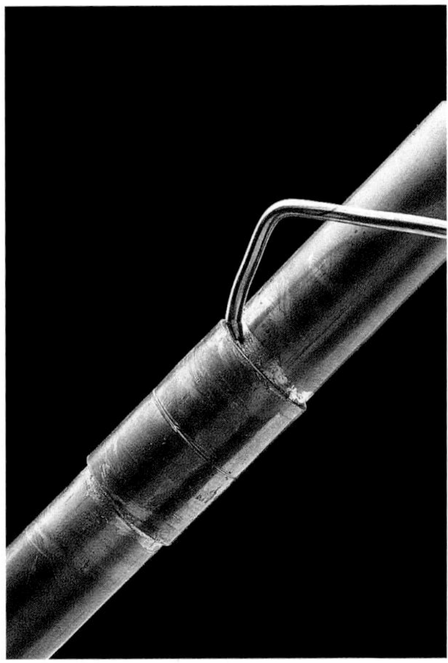

E. *Push ½" to ¾" of solder into each joint, allowing capillary action to draw liquefied solder into the joint.*

F. *When the joint has cooled, wipe away excess solder with a dry rag. Be careful: pipes will be hot.*

Working with Hypertufa

Hypertufa is wonderfully suited to building garden ornaments. There are many recipes available, and some are more reliable than others. Experience leads me to prefer these two recipes. Recipe #1, which contains fiberglass fibers, is ideal for producing lightweight, durable, medium-to-large planting containers. Recipe #2, which contains sand, is especially appropriate for smaller items and those that must hold water.

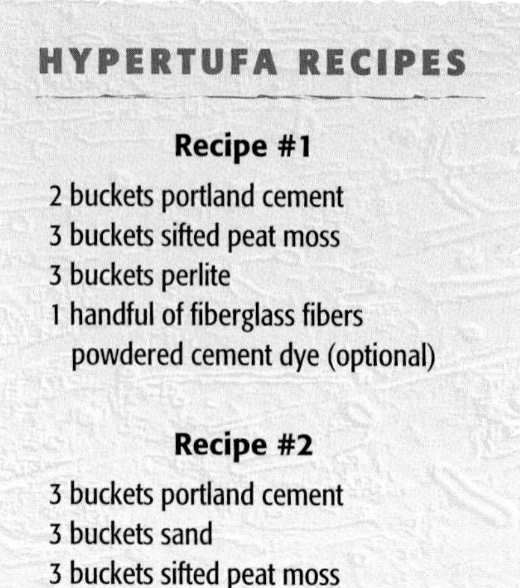

HYPERTUFA RECIPES

Recipe #1

2 buckets portland cement
3 buckets sifted peat moss
3 buckets perlite
1 handful of fiberglass fibers
powdered cement dye (optional)

Recipe #2

3 buckets portland cement
3 buckets sand
3 buckets sifted peat moss

The ingredients for both recipes are widely available at home and garden centers. Use portland cement rather than a prepared cement mix that contains gravel (which contributes unnecessary weight and gives the finished container a coarse texture). In Recipe #1, perlite, a soil lightener, takes the place of the aggregate typically found in concrete. For Recipe #2, use fine-textured mason's sand—it produces a stronger container than coarser grades of sand.

Peat moss naturally includes a range of textures, some of which are too coarse for hypertufa. Sifting the peat moss through hardware cloth takes care of that problem. If you plan to make several hypertufa pieces, it's most efficient to buy a large bale of peat moss, sift the entire bale, then store the sifted material for use over time.

The fiberglass fibers in Recipe #1 contribute strength to the mixture. This product is available at most building centers, but if you have trouble locating it, try a concrete or masonry supply center.

Hypertufa dries to the color of concrete. If you prefer another color, simply add a powdered concrete dye during the mixing process. Tinting products are very effective, so start with a small amount and add more if necessary.

HOW TO MAKE HYPERTUFA

Step A: Sift the Peat Moss

Place the hardware cloth across a large bucket or wheelbarrow. Rub the peat moss across the hardware cloth, sifting it through the mesh. Discard any debris or large particles.

The materials for making hypertufa are inexpensive and widely available. They include portland cement, perlite, peat moss, fiberglass fibers, mason's sand, concrete dye, hardware cloth, a plastic tarp, a dust mask, and gloves.

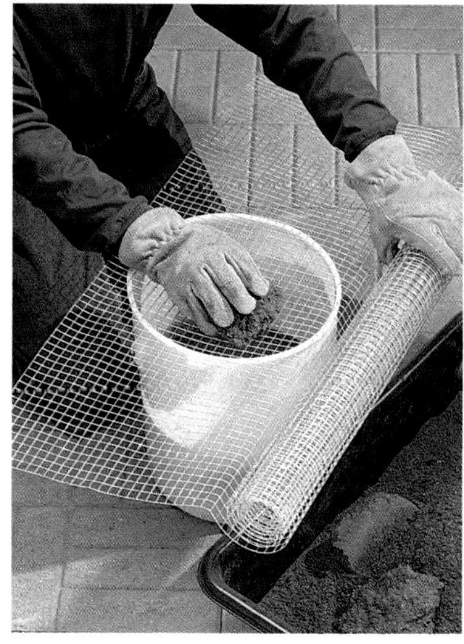

A. *Sift the peat moss through hardware cloth to remove any debris or large particles and break up clumps.*

Step B: Mix the Ingredients

1. Measure the cement, peat moss, and perlite or sand, and add them to a mixing trough or wheelbarrow. Using a hoe or small shovel, blend these ingredients thoroughly. If you're using Recipe #1, add the fiberglass fibers and mix again. Add concrete dye, if desired, and mix until the fiberglass fibers and the dye powder are evenly distributed throughout.

2. Add water and blend thoroughly. The amount of water required varies, so add a little at a time. It's easy to add more, but very difficult to correct the situation after you've added too much. The hypertufa is ready to be molded when you can squeeze a few drops of water from a handful.

Step C: Form the Hypertufa

1. Build forms from 2" polystyrene insulation (see individual projects). Secure joints with 2½" deck screws, and reinforce them with gaffer's tape. If the piece is a planting container, be sure to provide adequate drainage holes.

2. Pack the hypertufa into the form and firmly tamp it down. Continue adding and tamping until hypertufa reaches the recommended depth or fills the form (see individual projects).

3. Cover the project with plastic, and let it dry for 48 hours.

4. Disassemble the forms and remove the piece.

Step D: Shape & Cure the Piece

1. Sculpt the appearance of the piece by knocking off the corners and sharp edges. Add texture to the sides of the piece by using a paint scraper or screwdriver to scrape grooves into them. Finally, brush the surface with a wire brush.

2. Wrap the piece in plastic, and put it in a cool place to cure for about a month. Remember, the longer the hypertufa cures, the stronger it will be.

3. Unwrap the piece and let it cure outside, uncovered. If you're building a planter, let it cure for several weeks, periodically rinsing it with water to remove some of the alkalinity, which could harm plants that are grown in the container. Adding vinegar to the rinse water speeds this process, .

After the planter has cured outside for several weeks, move it inside, away from any sources of moisture, to cure for another week or so.

4. The fiberglass fibers in Recipe #1 produce a hairy fringe. Make sure pieces made from this recipe are dry, and then use a propane torch to burn off the fringe. Move the torch quickly, holding it in each spot no more than a second or two. If pockets of moisture remain, they may get hot enough to explode, leaving pot holes in the piece.

5. Apply a coat of masonry sealer to basins or other pieces that must hold water.

B. *Measure the ingredients into a mixing container and blend thoroughly. Add water, a little at a time, and mix.*

C. *Pack the hypertufa into the forms, and tamp it firmly. Cover the project with plastic, and let it cure for 48 hours.*

D. *Let the piece cure. Rinse it repeatedly; let it dry completely. Use a propane torch to burn off any fiberglass fibers.*

Building with Bricks

Bricks are easy to work with if you have the right tools and use good techniques. Before starting a brick project, plan carefully, evaluate the bricks you're using, and practice handling them. When working with bricks, wear gloves to protect your hands whenever possible. And always wear eye protection when cutting or splitting bricks, or any other masonry units, whether by hand or with a saw.

With bricks, as with any building material, planning minimizes problems during construction. Remember that you need to build a frost footing if the proposed brick structure is more than 3 ft. tall or if it will be tied to another permanent structure. Frost footings should extend about 12" past the frost line in your area.

Don't add mortar joint thickness to the total dimensions when you're planning a brick project. The actual size of a brick is ⅜" smaller than the nominal size, which allows for ⅜"-wide mortar joints. For example, a 9" (nominal) brick actually measures 8⅝", so four 9" bricks set with ⅜" mortar joints will measure 36" in length. To make sure planned dimensions work, test project layouts using ⅜" spacers between bricks. Whenever possible, make plans that use whole bricks, eliminating extensive cutting.

You'll need to learn a few brick-handling skills before you begin building projects. Even after you've learned these skills, be sure to buy extra bricks for every project. Bricks vary in density and the type of materials used to make them, which greatly affects how they respond to cutting and the way they absorb moisture. You'll always need to make practice cuts on a sample and test the water absorption rate to determine their density before you begin a project.

To test the absorption rate of a brick, use an eyedropper to drop 20 drops of water onto one spot and check it after 60 seconds. If the surface is completely dry, dampen the bricks with water before you lay them. Otherwise, they'll wick the moisture out of the mortar before it has a chance to set properly.

HOW TO MARK & CUT BRICKS

Step A: Mark Straight Cutting Lines

When you can't avoid cutting bricks, the first thing you have to do is mark the cuts. If you're making many identical cuts, use a T-square and pencil to mark groups of bricks at the same time. Align the ends and hold the bricks in place as you mark.

A. *Use a T-square and pencil to mark several bricks for cutting. Make sure the ends of the bricks are all aligned.*

B. *Use a circular saw with a masonry-cutting blade to score a group of bricks. Clamp the bricks together, ends aligned.*

C. *To split a brick, align a mason's chisel with the scored line. Tap on the chisel with a hammer until the brick splits.*

Step B: Score Straight Cuts

1. To avoid cracking them, set the bricks on a bed of sand as you work. If the cutting line falls over the core, score the brick on two sides; if it falls over the web area, score all four sides.

2. For small jobs, use a mason's chisel and hammer both to score and to cut the bricks. To score a brick, use a hammer to tap on the mason's chisel, leaving cut marks ⅛" to ¼" deep. For large jobs, you can ensure uniformity and speed up the process by scoring the bricks with a circular saw and a masonry-cutting blade. Set the saw's blade depth between ⅛" and ¼". Carefully align the ends of the bricks, and clamp them securely at each end, using pipe clamps or bar clamps.

Step C: Make Straight Cuts

Use a mason's chisel and a hammer to split the bricks. Hold the chisel at a slight angle and tap it firmly with the hammer.

Step D: Mark Angled Cuts

Set the bricks in position, allowing ⅜" for mortar joints, where necessary. Mark cutting lines, using a straightedge to make sure the cutting lines are straight and accurate.

Step E: Score Angled Cuts

Making angled cuts is a gradual process—to avoid ruining the brick you have to make a series of cuts that move toward the final cutting line. First, score a straight line in the waste area of the brick, about ⅛" away from the starting point of the marked cutting

TIP: USING A BRICK SPLITTER

If your project requires many cuts, it's a good idea to rent a brick splitter, a tool that makes accurate, consistent cuts in bricks and pavers. Always read and follow manufacturer's instructions on a rental tool, and refer questions to the rental center.

In general, though, a brick splitter is easy to use. Just mark a cutting line, and then set the brick on the table of the splitter. Align the cutting line on the brick with the cutting blade on the splitter.

Once the brick is in position on the splitter table, pull down sharply on the handle. The cutting blade will cleave the brick along the cutting line.

Note: *Always wear eye protection when cutting masonry products, including bricks and pavers.*

D. *To mark angled cuts, set the bricks in position and mark the exact angle of the cut, using a pencil and a straightedge.*

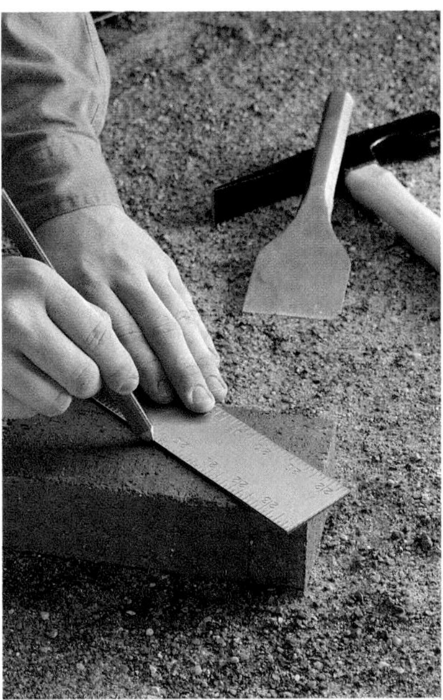

E. *Mark a line in the waste area of the brick, about ⅛" away from the starting point of the cutting line.*

F. *Make a series of cuts, gradually removing angled sections until all of the waste area is removed.*

line and perpendicular to the side of the brick.

Step F: Complete Angled Cuts

To make the remaining cuts, keep the chisel stationary at the point of the first cut. Pivot it slightly; score and split again. Keep the pivot point of the chisel at the edge of the brick. Repeat the process until all of the waste area is removed.

HOW TO MIX AND THROW MORTAR

Mixing the mortar properly is critical to the success of a brick project. If the mortar's too thick, it falls off the trowel in a heap. If it's too watery, it's impossible to control. Finding the perfect water ratio calls for experimentation. Mix only as much mortar as you can use within about 30 minutes—once mortar begins to set up, it's difficult to work with and yields poor results.

Step A: Mix the Mortar

1. Empty the mortar mix into a mortar box or wheelbarrow and form a depression in the center. Pour about three-fourths of the recommended amount of water into the depression, and then mix it in with a masonry hoe. Be careful not to overwork the mix. Continue mixing in small amounts of water until the mortar clings to a trowel just long enough for you to deliver it in a controlled, even line that holds its shape after settling. Take careful notes on how much water you add to each batch, and record the ratios for the best mixture.

2. Set a piece of plywood on blocks at a convenient height, and place a shovelful of mortar on the surface. Slice off a strip of mortar from the pile, using the edge of a mason's trowel. Slip the trowel, point-first, under the section of mortar and lift up. Snap the trowel gently downward to dislodge any excess mortar clinging to the edges. A good load of mortar is enough to set three bricks. Don't get too far ahead of yourself—if you throw too much at one time, it will set up before you're ready.

Step B: Throw the Mortar

Position the trowel at your starting point. In one motion, begin turning your wrist over, and quickly move the trowel across the surface to spread the mortar consistently along the bricks. Don't worry if you don't get this right the first time. Throwing mortar is a quick, smooth technique that takes time to perfect, but even a beginning bricklayer can successfully use the basic technique in pretty short order. Keep practicing until you can consistently throw a rounded line about 2½" wide and about 2 ft. long.

Step C: Furrow the Mortar Line

Drag the point of the trowel through the center of the mortar line in a slight back-and-forth motion. This action, called "furrowing," helps distribute the mortar evenly.

A. *Mix mortar to the proper consistency. Place a shovelful on a plywood work surface, and slice off a strip of mortar.*

B. *Throw the mortar in a rounded line about 2½" wide and about 2 ft. long.*

C. *"Furrow" the mortar line by dragging the point of the trowel through its center, using a slight back-and-forth motion.*

TIP: BUTTER YOUR BRICKS

"Buttering" is a term used to describe the process of applying mortar to a brick before adding it to the structure being built. To butter a brick, apply a heavy layer of mortar to one end, then cut off the excess with a trowel.

HOW TO LAY BRICKS

Step A: Mark Reference Lines & Lay the First Course

1. Before you can lay any bricks, you have to create a sturdy, level building surface. So, first pour a footing or slab, as required for your project (see page 93), and let that concrete cure.
2. Dry-lay the first course of bricks, centered on the footing or slab, using a ⅜"-diameter dowel for spacing. Mark reference lines around the bricks.
3. Dampen the footing or slab with water, and dampen the bricks if necessary (see page 106).
4. Mix mortar and throw a bed of mortar inside the reference lines. Butter the inside end of the first brick. Press this brick into the mortar, creating a ⅜" mortar bed. Cut away the excess mortar.
5. Plumb the face of the end brick, using a level. Tap lightly with the handle of the trowel to adjust the brick if it's not plumb. Level the brick end to end.
6. Butter the end of a second brick, and then set it into the mortar bed, pushing it toward the first brick to create a joint of ⅜". Continue to butter and place bricks, using the reference lines as a guide and following the plans for the specific project.

Step B: Check Your Work with a Level

Add courses, frequently checking your work with a level to make sure it's both level and plumb. Adjust any bricks that are misaligned by tapping them lightly with the handle of the trowel.

Step C: Tool the Joints & Complete the Project

Every 30 minutes, stop laying bricks and tool all joints that have hardened enough to resist minimal finger pressure. Tooling joints involves drawing a jointing tool across each joint in a fluid motion to smooth away excess mortar. Tool the horizontal joints first, then the vertical ones. Use a trowel to cut away any excess mortar you pressed from the joints. When the mortar is set, but not completely hardened, brush any excess off the faces of the bricks.

A. *Dry-lay the first course and mark reference lines. Then lay a bed of mortar, butter the bricks, and begin laying them.*

B. *Frequently check your work with a level; adjust bricks as necessary.*

C. *Every 30 minutes, smooth the joints, using a jointing tool.*

Adding a Garden GFCI Receptacle

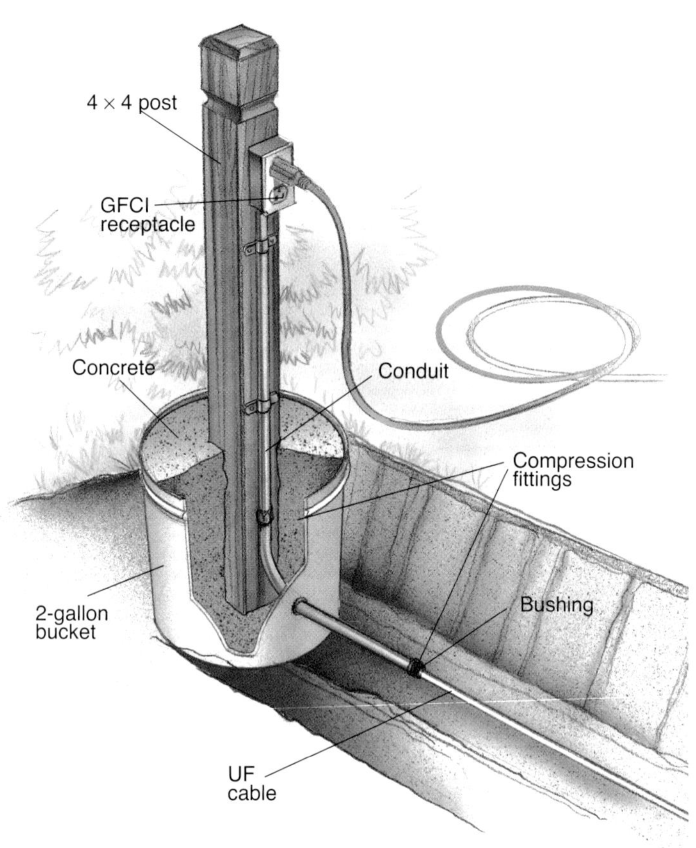

A GFCI (ground-fault circuit interrupter) receptacle can be added to any outdoor room to help with a variety of tasks, including providing electricity for fountains or low-voltage lighting systems.

The following sequence illustrates a basic method for creating a freestanding receptacle anchored to a wood post embedded in a bucket of concrete. The receptacle is wired with UF (underground feeder) cable running through a trench from a junction box inside the house or garage. Sections of conduit protect the outdoor cable where it's exposed.

If you'd like to attach the outlet to an existing landscape structure, such as a deck or fence, modify the project by attaching the receptacle box and conduit to that structure. Keep in mind that freestanding receptacles should be at least 12", but no more than 18", above ground level.

Before you begin this project, have your inspector review your plans and issue a work permit. Inspectors rely on the National Electrical Code (NEC) as well as local Codes that address climate and soil conditions in the region. If local Code requires that your work be inspected, schedule those visits at the appropriate points during the project.

HOW TO INSTALL A GARDEN RECEPTACLE

Step A: Install the LB Connector & Conduit

1. Plan a route from an indoor junction box to the

A. *Drill a hole through the wall, and mount an LB connector. Assemble a length of conduit and sweep fitting.*

B. *Assemble and attach the receptacle box and conduit to the post. Add concrete to anchor the assembly in the bucket.*

TOOLS & MATERIALS

- Wire cutters
- Utility knife
- Fish tape
- Wire strippers
- LB connector
- Metal sweeps
- 1" metal conduit (6 ft.)
- Compression fittings
- Plastic bushings
- Pipe straps
- 2-gallon bucket
- 4-ft. 4 × 4 post
- Metal outdoor receptacle box
- Concrete mix
- UF cable
- GFCI receptacle
- Wire connectors
- Cable staples
- Grounding pigtail

location for the GFCI. Drill a 1"-diameter hole through an exterior wall, near the junction box.

2. Mark the underground cable run from this hole to the receptacle location. Remove sod and dig a trench, 8" to 12" wide and at least 12" deep, along the marked route.

3. Install the LB connector on the outside of the hole. Measure and cut a length of conduit about 4" shorter than the distance from the LB connector to the bottom of the trench. Attach the conduit to a sweep fitting, using a compression fitting. Attach a plastic bushing to the open end of the sweep to keep its metal edges from damaging the cable.

4. Attach the conduit assembly to the bottom of the LB connector; then anchor the conduit to the wall, using pipe straps.

5. Cut a length of conduit to extend from the LB connector through the wall to the inside of the house. Attach the conduit to the LB connector from inside the house, and then attach a plastic bushing to the open end of the conduit.

Step B: Assemble & Install the Receptacle Post

1. Drill or cut a 1½" hole through the side of a 2-gallon plastic bucket, near the bottom.

2. Mount the receptacle box to the post with galvanized screws. Position the post in the bucket.

3. Measure and cut a length of conduit to run from the receptacle box to a point 4" above the base of the bucket. Attach the conduit to the receptacle box, and mount it to the post, using pipe straps.

4. Insert a conduit sweep through the hole in the bucket, and attach it to the end of the conduit, using a compression fitting. Thread a plastic bushing onto the open end of the sweep.

5. Dig a hole at the end of the trench. Place the bucket and post into the hole; fill the bucket with concrete and let it dry completely.

Step C: Lay the UF Cable

1. Measure the distance from the junction box in the house out to the receptacle box. Cut a length of UF cable 2 ft. longer than this measurement. At each end of the cable, use a utility knife to pare away 8" of the outer sheathing.

2. Lay the cable along the bottom of the trench

***C.** Measure and cut UF cable, and lay it in the trench. Use a fish tape to pull the cable up into the LB connector.*

***D.** Using the fish tape, pull the cable through the conduit and up into the receptacle box.*

from the house to the receptacle location.

3. Open the cover on the LB connector and feed a fish tape through the conduit and out of the sweep. Feed the wires at the end of the UF cable through the loop in the fish tape, and then wrap electrical tape around the wires up to the sheathing.

4. Using the fish tape, carefully pull the end of the cable up through the conduit to the LB connector.

Step D: Fishing the UF Cable to the Receptacle Box

1. At the other end of the trench, feed the fish tape down through the conduit and out of the sweep.

2. Attach the exposed wires to the loop in the fish tape, and secure them with electrical tape.

3. Pull the cable through the conduit up into the receptacle box until about ½" of cable sheathing extends into the box.

Step E: Connect the Receptacle

1. Using wire strippers, remove ¾" of the insulation around the two insulated wires extending into the receptacle box.

2. Attach a bare copper pigtail to the grounding terminal on the back of the receptacle box. Join the two bare copper wires to the green grounding lead attached to the GFCI, using a wire connector.

3. Connect the black circuit wire to the brass screw terminal marked LINE on the GFCI. Connect the white wire to the silver terminal marked LINE.

4. Carefully tuck all wires into the receptacle box, and mount the receptacle. Install the cover plate.

Step F: Connect the Cable at the Junction Box

1. From inside the house, extend the fish tape through the conduit and LB connector. Attach the cable wires to the fish tape loop, and pull the cable into the house. Anchor the cable along framing members, using wire staples.

2. ***Turn off the power to the circuit serving the junction box.*** Remove the junction box cover and use a neon circuit tester to confirm that the power is off.

3. Use a screwdriver to open a knockout in the side of the junction box. Pull the end of the UF cable into the box through the knockout, and secure it with a cable clamp. About ½" of the outer sheathing should extend into the box, and the individual wires should be about 8" long. (Cut excess wire down to size.)

4. Using a wire stripper, remove ¾" of insulation from the insulated wires.

5. Unscrew the wire connector attached to the bare copper grounding wires inside the box. Position the new grounding wire alongside the existing wires, and replace the wire connector.

6. Using the same technique, connect the new black wire to the existing black wires, and connect the new white wire to the existing white wires.

7. Replace the junction box cover, and restore power to the circuit.

8. Fill the trench and replace the sod.

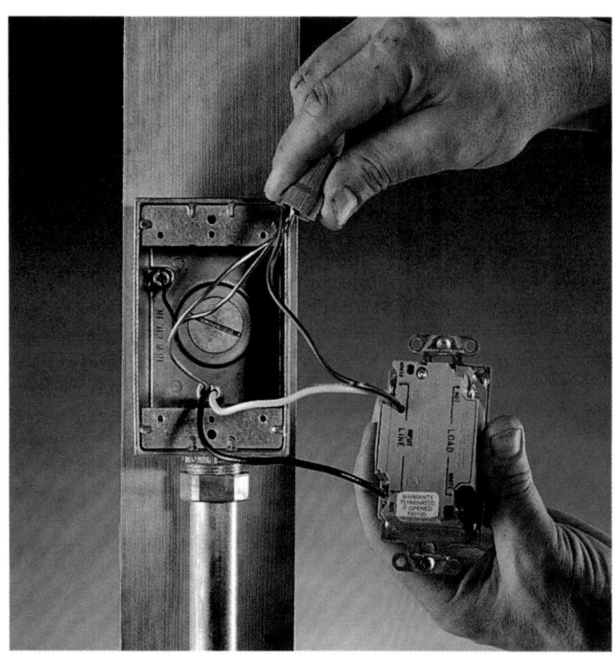

E. *Join the grounding wires; connect the black wire to the brass LINE terminal, and the white wire to the silver LINE terminal.*

F. *Extend the UF cable into the junction box. Connect the new wires to the existing wires, using wire connectors.*

MATERIALS SOURCES

Mist maker (page 15)
Fountains of Tranquility
1-800-229-3376

Hinge pin bushing (page 16)
Motormite Mfg. Div. of R&B, Inc.
P.O. Box 1800
Colmar, PA 18915-1800

½" brass cross (page 86)
NIBCO
1516 Middlebury Street
Elkhart, IN 46515-1167
1-800-234-0227

HELPFUL WEB SITES
www.birdsforever.com
www.duncraft.com
www.garden.com

CONVERTING MEASUREMENTS

To Convert:	To:	Multiply by:
Inches	Millimeters	25.4
Inches	Centimeters	2.54
Feet	Meters	0.305
Yards	Meters	0.914
Square inches	Square centimeters	6.45
Square feet	Square meters	0.093
Square yards	Square meters	0.836
Cubic inches	Cubic centimeters	16.4
Cubic feet	Cubic meters	0.0283
Cubic yards	Cubic meters	0.765
Ounces	Milliliters	30.0
Pints (U.S.)	Liters	0.473 (Imp. 0.568)
Quarts (U.S.)	Liters	0.946 (Imp. 1.136)
Gallons (U.S.)	Liters	3.785 (Imp. 4.546)
Ounces	Grams	28.4
Pounds	Kilograms	0.454

To Convert:	To:	Multiply by:
Millimeters	Inches	0.039
Centimeters	Inches	0.394
Meters	Feet	3.28
Meters	Yards	1.09
Square centimeters	Square inches	0.155
Square meters	Square feet	10.8
Square meters	Square yards	1.2
Cubic centimeters	Cubic inches	0.061
Cubic meters	Cubic feet	35.3
Cubic meters	Cubic yards	1.31
Milliliters	Ounces	.033
Liters	Pints (U.S.)	2.114 (Imp. 1.76)
Liters	Quarts (U.S.)	1.057 (Imp. 0.88)
Liters	Gallons (U.S.)	0.264 (Imp. 0.22)
Grams	Ounces	0.035
Kilograms	Pounds	2.2

Index